D0991686

Knitting
for
Little Feet

Knitting for Little Feet:

40 Booties, Socks, and Slippers for Babies and Kids

T

S

Trafalgar Square

North Pomfret, Vermont

First published in the United States of America in 2011 by
Trafalgar Square Books
North Pomfret, Vermont 05053

Printed in China

Originally published in Germany as Für kleine Füße stricken

This edition is published by arrangement with Claudia Böhme Rights & Literary Agency,
Hannover, Germany (www.agency-boehme.com)

ISBN: 978-1-57076-478-3

Library of Congress Control Number: 2010943262

We wish to thank the companies Coats LLC, Kensingen, www.coatsgmbh.de for the support
of this book.
DESIGNS: Nadja Brandt (pp 49-51, 54, 55, 60-65, 90, 91, 94, 95), Coats LLC (pp 8-11,
14-17, 20-23, 30, 31, 46-48, 52/53, 56-59, 88/89), Friederike Pfund (pp 32-37, 74/75,
92/93, 108-113), Mathilde Putra (pp 76-85), Barbara Sander (pp 66-69, 106/107), Lilja
Sommer (pp 70/71, 96-101), Helga Spitz (pp 12/13, 18/19, 24-29, 38-43, 86/87), Stephanie
van der Linden (pp 102-105)
PROJECT MANAGEMENT: Dr. Ulrike Voigt
LAYOUT: Petra Theilfarth
PHOTOS: Frechverlag GmbH, 70499 Stuttgart; Photography Studio: Ullrich and Co.,
Renningen (pp 102-105, 116, 117, 119, 120, 121 right column, 122, 125, 127); Light View
GmbH, Jochen Frank, Laichingen (pp 1-18, 20-33, 38-101. 106-111, lighting Michael
Ruder, Stuttgart (pp 19, 35-37, 113, 114, 118/119, 121 left column); Sabine Münch, Berlin
(pp 123/124)

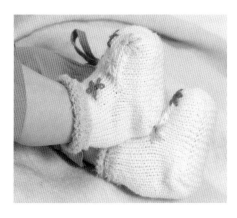

Welcome to the World

BOOTIES AND SOCKS FOR THE WEE ONES

The best thing you can give babies is warmth and affection. How wonderful when that warmth is also creative and beautiful! Whether you choose a simple pattern of knits and purls, or a more challenging pattern with flowers, checks, lace or a crocheted edge, each magical design will be a joy to knit. Who knows, a pair might even make an appearance at a christening! These small sizes make it easy to finish many projects in no time.

Scrumptious

LEVEL OF DIFFICULTY
Easy

SIZES
0-3 months (approx)

3 (3¼, 3¾) in / 7.5 (8.5, 9.5) cm

The instructions for the first size are given before the parentheses; those for the second and third sizes are in order within the parentheses. If only one number is given, it applies to all sizes.

MATERIALS
Yarn: Schachenmayr Baby Wool (100% Merino wool, 25 g, 93 yds / 85 m) Light Blue (54)

Needles: set of 4 or 5 dpn U.S. sizes 1.5 – 4 / 2.5 – 3.5 mm

GAUGE
28 sts and 36 rows in stockinette = 4 x 4 in / 10 x 10 cm.

Adjust needle size to obtain correct gauge.

STITCH PATTERNS

RIBBING
Repeat (p1, k3).

STOCKINETTE
Worked back and forth: Knit on RS and purl on WS.
In the round: Knit all rounds.

INSTRUCTIONS

Cast on 28 (32, 36) sts and join, being careful not to twist cast-on row.
Rnds 1-2: Knit.
Rnd 3-5: Purl.
Rnds 6-7: Knit.
Work Rnds 3-7 two more times = 17 rounds total.

Work in ribbing for 1½ in / 4 cm and then work the Short row heel (see page 118). Work the instep in ribbing on ndls 2 and 3. Work the rest of the sts in stockinette on ndls 1 and 4. When foot is desired length, finish with a band toe (see page 121).

Make the other sock the same way.

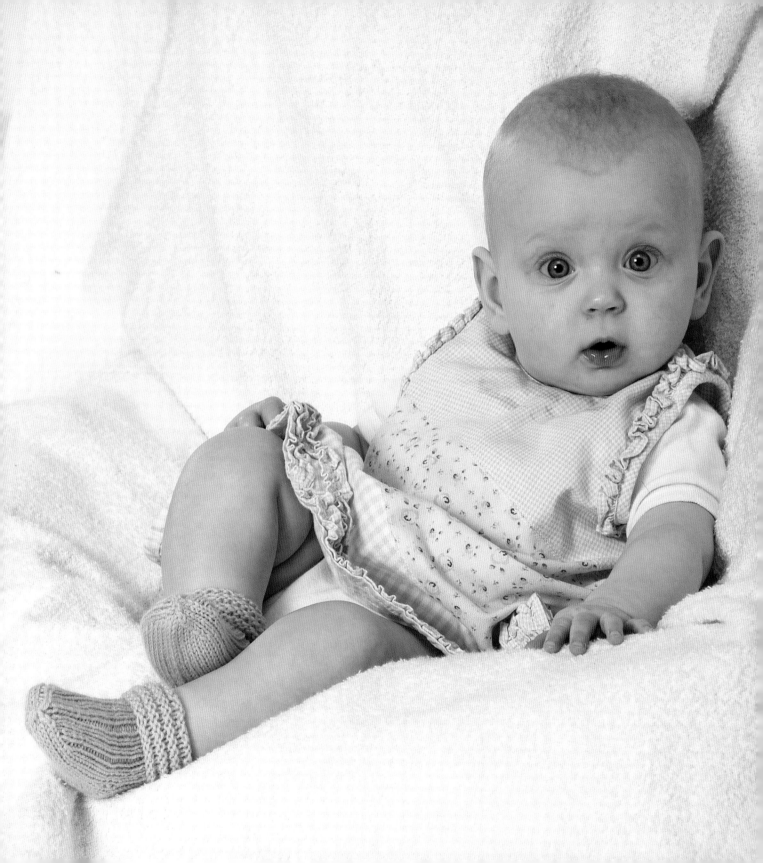

Rainbow Bright

LEVEL OF DIFFICULTY
Easy

SIZES
0-6 months (approx)

2¾ (3¼, 3½, 4, 4¼) in / 7 (8, 9, 10, 11) cm

The instructions for the first size are given before the parentheses; those for the second through fourth sizes are in order within the parentheses. If only one number is given, it applies to all sizes.

MATERIALS
Yarn: Schachenmayr Baby Soft (60% Acrylic/40% nylon, 25 g, 77 yds / 70 m) (enough for a pair in any of the sizes above)

Color suggestions: Denim (152), Cherry (130), Green (170), Pink (136), Blue (153), or Rose (135).

Notions: Ribbon, buttons, or contrast color yarn.

Needles: U.S. sizes 2.5 – 6 / 3 – 4 mm

GAUGE
22 sts and 30 rows in stockinette = 4 x 4 in / 10 x 10 cm.

Adjust needle size to obtain correct gauge.

STITCH PATTERNS

STOCKINETTE
Worked back and forth: Knit on RS and purl on WS.

GARTER STITCH
Knit every row.

INSTRUCTIONS

Begin bootie with the sole. CO 32 (36, 40, 44, 48) sts and work back and forth in stockinette for 1¼ (1½, 1½, 1½, 1½) in / 3 (4, 4, 4, 4) cm. End with a WS (purl) row. Now begin shaping for upper foot:

Row 1: K14 (16, 18, 20, 22), k2tog, ssk, k14 (16, 18, 20, 22) = 30 (34, 38, 42, 46) sts remain.
Row 2 and all other WS rows: Purl.
Row 3: K13 (15, 17, 19, 21), k2tog, ssk, k13 (15, 17, 19, 21) = 28 (32, 36, 40, 44) sts rem.

Continue shaping the foot on RS rows the same way until a total of 22 (26, 30, 34, 38) sts rem. For the lace hole row at ankle: P2tog, *yo, p2tog; rep from * across until 2 sts rem; end p2tog = 22 (26, 30, 34, 38) sts.
Now work in garter st for 8 (8, 10, 10, 12) rows and then BO.

Make the other bootie the same way.

FINISHING
Seam the shoes along center back and under the foot. Decorate the shoes with ribbons, bows, or buttons. Make a twisted cord about 15¾ in / 40 cm long for each shoe and thread through lace holes at ankle.

SMALL BOW
CO 6 sts and knit 19 rows in garter stitch. BO. Cut a long piece of yarn and tie piece at the center, tightening yarn to shape the bow. Sew to front of shoe as shown in photo.

Here Comes a Butterfly ...

LEVEL OF DIFFICULTY
Intermediate

SIZE
0 – 6 months (approx)

(see page 127 for size measurements)

MATERIALS
Yarn: Schachenmayr Baby Wool (100%
Merino wool, 25 g, 93 yds / 85 m) Purple (49),
Pink (36), pale Rose (35)

Needles: set of 4 or 5 dpn U.S. size 2.5 / 3 mm

GAUGE
28 sts and 36 rows in stockinette = 4 x 4 in /
10 x 10 cm.

Adjust needle size to obtain correct gauge.

STITCH PATTERNS

GARTER STITCH
Garter Stitch in the Round: Alternately knit 1 rnd,
purl 1 rnd.

STOCKINETTE
Stockinette in the Round: Knit all rounds.

STRIPE SEQUENCE
2 rnds purple, 2 rnds pink, 2 rnds rose. Repeat
this sequence.

INSTRUCTIONS

Begin with the sole. With pink, CO 36 sts; divide
sts evenly over dpn and join, being careful not to
twist cast-on row. Work in garter stitch in the
round. On the 3rd round, increase 1 stitch each at
the beginning of needles 1 and 3 and at the end
of needles 2 and 4. Repeat these increases 3

times on every other round = 52 stitches.
Continue working garter stitch in the round following the stripe sequence above. After completing 20 rnds stripe pattern, work 8 rnds with pink
as follows:
Rnd 1: K14, (k2tog) 12 times, k14 = 40 sts remain.
Rnd 2: Purl around.
Rnd 3: K14, (k2tog) 6 times, k14.
Rnd 4: Purl around.
Now work 4 rounds in garter stitch with pink and
then 4 rnds with rose. Next, work 8 rnds garter
stitch with purple and then BO all sts. Seam the
sole and then weave in all tails neatly on WS.

KNITTED ROSE

With purple, CO 8 sts. Purl 1 row. On the next
row, increase with (k1, p1, k1) into every stitch.
On the following row, BO all sts knitwise. Roll
the piece into a rose shape and secure to front of
bootie with a few stitches.

Make the other bootie the same way.

Let's See Your Little Feet

LEVEL OF DIFFICULTY
Experienced

SIZES
0-3 months (approx)

3 (3¼, 3¾) in / 7.5 (8.5, 9.5) cm

The instructions for the first size are given before the parentheses; those for the second and third sizes are in order within the parentheses. If only one number is given, it applies to all sizes.

MATERIALS
Yarn: Regia 4-ply (75% wool/25% polyamide, 50 g, 230 yds / 210 m) Sweet (1402), Bubblegum (1401), and White (600).

Needles: set of 4 or 5 dpn U.S. sizes 0-2.5 / 2-3 mm

GAUGE
30 sts and 42 rows or rounds in stockinette = 4 x 4 in / 10 x 10 cm.

Adjust needle size to obtain correct gauge.

STITCH PATTERNS

GARTER STITCH
Worked back and forth: Knit all rows.

STOCKINETTE
Worked back and forth: Knit on RS and purl on WS.
In the round: Knit all rounds.

INSTRUCTIONS

The wrap for the leg is worked back and forth in two pieces. Each half begins at the center back of the leg.
Begin the first half of the wrap by casting on 30 (34, 38) sts with white. Knit the first row. On the next, WS, row, purl 28 (32, 36), k2. Continue, working the first two stitches in garter st for top edging on leg and the remainder of the stitches in stockinette.

Mark the placement of the heel on row 5: place markers around the 20th (22nd, 24th) st. Slip the marked stitch together with the stitch before it. Knit the next st and then pass the slipped sts over it = 28 (32, 36) sts rem. On every RS row work the double decrease the same way. Repeat the decrease 7 (9, 11) times = 14 sts for a total of 19 (23, 27) rows − 1¾ (2¼, 2½) in / 4.5 (5.5, 6.5) cm. Now continue, working 2 sts at each side in garter st and the center 10 sts in stockinette. On each of the next 10 RS rows, work until 4 sts remain, sl 1 knitwise-k1-psso, k2; 4 sts rem after all decreases.

Now work an I-cord over these 4 sts: *do not turn, slip the sts back to front of dpn and knit them, tightening working yarn on first st to keep the cord rounded; repeat from * until cord is 5½ in / 14 cm long. Cut yarn and bring tail through rem sts. To make a tassel for the end of the cord, cut a piece of white yarn about 3 in / 8 cm long, fold it in half, and thread it through the end of the I-cord. Wrap top of tassel with tail yarn to secure. Trim tassel to ¾ in / 2 cm.

For the second half of the wrap, use Sweet or Bubblegum to pick up and knit 30 (34, 38) sts in the cast-on row of the first half and work the second half to correspond to first half.

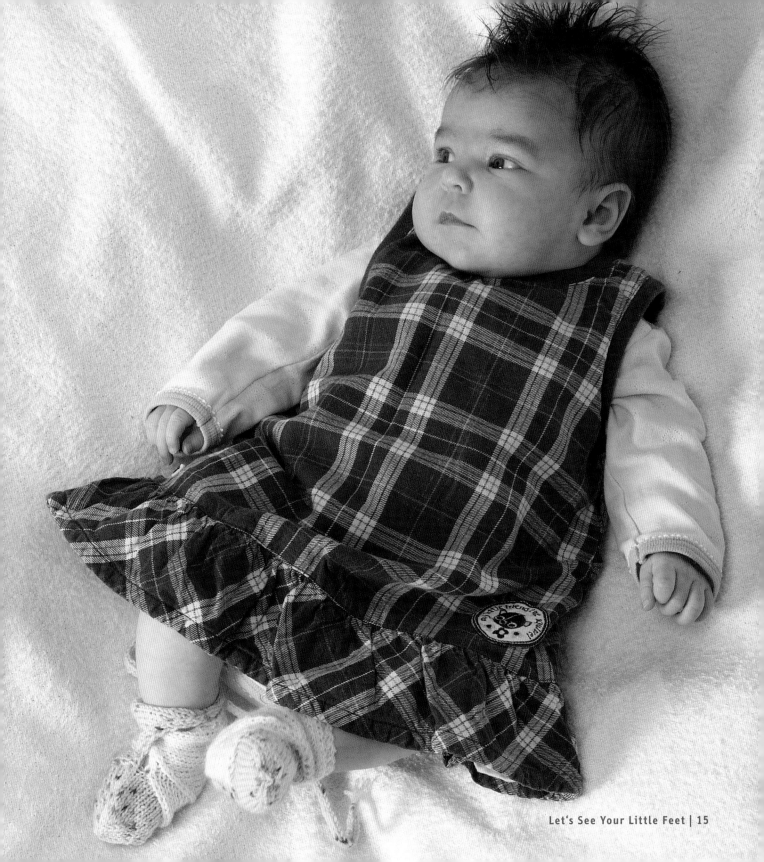

... Let's See Your Little Feet

Begin the foot at the front with Sweet or Bubblegum, pick up and knit 14 (16, 18) at the beg of garter stitch edge of wrap and then along the edge of the second half. Divide sts evenly onto 4 dpn = 7 (8, 9) sts on each needle. Continue around in stockinette. Work the band toe when piece is about 1 (1¼ 1½) in / 2.5 (3, 3.5) cm from the pick-up row. On ndls 1 and 3, knit until 3 sts rem on ndl, k2tog and knit last st. On ndls 2 and 4, knit the first st and then k2tog, knit rem sts. Repeat these decreases on the 3rd round 1 time, on every other round 2 times, and then on every round until 8 sts remain. Cut yarn and pull tail through rem sts; pull tight and weave in tail on WS. The foot should be about 3¼ (3½, 4) in / 8 (9, 10) cm long.

Work the second sock as a mirror image of the first.

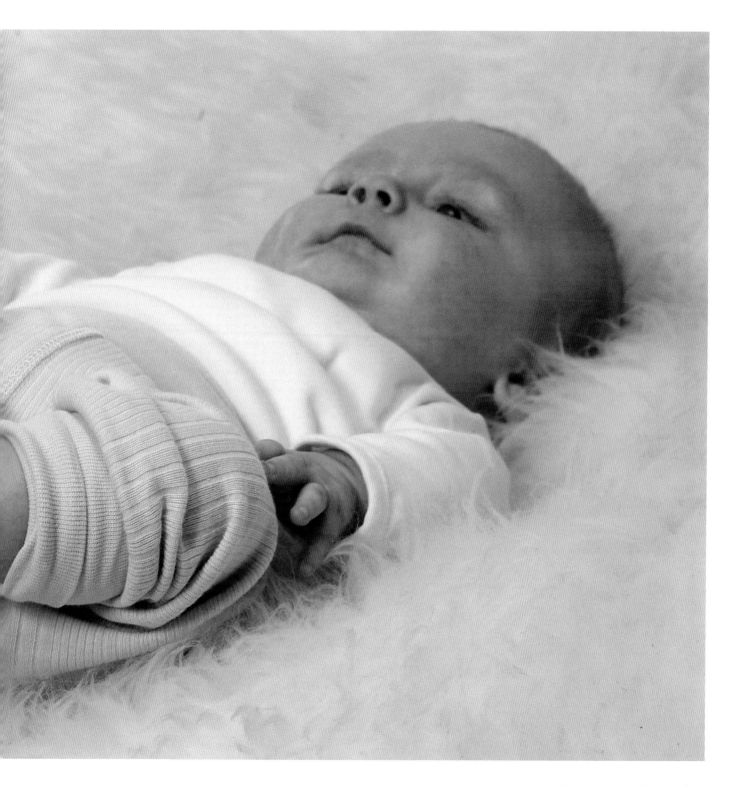

For Little Ladies

LEVEL OF DIFFICULTY
Experienced

SIZE
3-6 months (approx)
(see page 127 for size measurements)

MATERIALS
DK yarn

Yarn: Regia 6-ply silk, (55% wool/25% nylon/20% silk, 50 g, 136 yd / 124 m) Rose pink (035)

Needles: set of 4 or 5 dpn U.S. size 4 / 3.5 mm

Notions: 2 small buttons

GAUGE
22 sts and 30 rows in stockinette = 4 x 4 in / 10 x 10 cm.

Adjust needle size to obtain correct gauge.

STITCH PATTERNS

GARTER STITCH
Garter Stitch in the Round: Alternately knit 1 rnd, purl 1 rnd.
Garter Stitch back and forth: Knit all rows.

RIBBING:
K1, p1 around or across.

FISHERMAN'S RIB IN THE ROUND
Rnd 1: ^ K1, p1; rep from * around.
Rnd 2: * K1 into row below, p1; rep from * around.
Repeat rnds 1 and 2.

INSTRUCTIONS

Begin on the sole. CO 32 sts, divide sts evenly over dpn and join, being careful not to twist cast-on row.

Work garter stitch in the round. On rnd 3, begin increasing:

Ndls 1 and 3: M1 after the first st on ndl.

Ndls 2 and 4: M1 before the last st on ndl.

Increase the same way on every other rnd 3 more times = 48 sts.

Work 16 rnds in fisherman's rib and then continue in garter stitch as follows:

Rnd 1: K12, (k2tog) 12 times, k12 = 36 sts.

Rnd 2: Purl around.

Rnd 3: K12, (k2tog) 6 times, k12 = 30 sts.

Work in garter stitch for another 4 rnds. Next, work 5 rnds in ribbing.

Work back and forth in garter st (the space between ndls 2 and 3 is the center front) for 12 rows and then BO.

FINISHING
Sew on the button as shown in photo. Seam the sole and weave in all yarn tails on WS.

Make the other shoe the same way.

Little Tiny Diamonds

LEVEL OF DIFFICULTY
Experienced

SIZES
0-3 months (approx)

Foot length 3¼ (4) in / 8 (10) cm

The instructions for the 3¼ in / 8 cm foot are given before the parentheses; those for the 4 in / 10 cm length are within parentheses. If only one number is given, it applies to both sizes.

MATERIALS
Yarn: Regia 4-ply (75% wool/25% polyamide, 50 g, 230 yds / 210 m) Cherry (2002) or Royal blue (2000) = MC; 50 g ball or leftovers Pink (1976) or Fern (1092) = CC.

Needles: set of 4 or 5 dpn U.S. size 0-2.5 / 2-3 mm

GAUGE
Garter stitch: 30 sts and 60 rows = 4 x 4 in / 10 x 10 cm

Brioche: 26 sts and 56 rnds = 4 x 4 in / 10 x 10 cm

Two-color garter stitch: 30 sts and 68 rows = 4 x 4 in / 10 x 10 cm.

Adjust needle size to obtain correct gauge.

STITCH PATTERNS

GARTER STITCH
Knit every row.

BRIOCHE IN THE ROUND
Worked over an even number of sts.

Rnd 1: * K1, sl 1 purlwise, yo; rep from * around.

Rnd 2: * Sl 1 purlwise, yo, k2tog (previously slipped st and yarnover); rep from * around.

Rnd 3: * K2tog (slipped st + yo of previous rnd), sl 1, yo; rep from * around.

After working rnds 1-3 once, repeat rnds 2 and 3.

TWO-COLOR GARTER STITCH
Work back and forth over an even number of sts.

Rows 1 and 2 with MC: Knit.

Row 3 with CC: Edge st (knit), sl 1 purlwise wyb, * k1, sl 1 purlwise wyb; rep from * and end with edge st.

Row 4 with CC: Knit.

Row 5 with MC: Edge st, k1, * sl 1 purlwise wyb, k1; rep from * across and end with edge st.

Row 6 with MC: Knit.

After working rows 1-6 once, repeat rows 3-6.

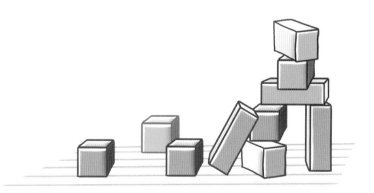

... Little Tiny Diamonds

INSTRUCTIONS

The sock begins on the sole with garter st worked back and forth over two ndls. With MC, cast on 22 (28) sts and work in garter st, beginning on WS. To round the sides, on the 4th and 8th rows, increase 1 st at each side = 26 (32) sts. When piece is about 2¼ (2³⁄₈) in / 5.5 (6) cm long (= 33 (35) rows) and on the following 4th row on RS knit the edge st together with the next st, knit to last 2 sts and k2tog = 22 (28) sts. When piece is 2³⁄₈ (2½) in / 6 (6.5) cm long, bind off all sts.

With MC, with ndl 1, pick up and knit 16 (18) sts along the rounding at the heel; with ndl 2, pick up and knit 18 (22) sts along the cast-on row; with ndl 3, pick up and knit 16 (18) sts on opposite side; with ndl 4, pick up and knit 18 (22) sts along bound-off row = 68 (80) sts. Now work brioche in the round for 1¼ (1½) in / 3 (3.5) cm = 17 (20) rounds. Where all the sts had previously been bound off, mark the 8th (9th) st on ndl 2 and the 11th (14th) st on ndl 4. Now the instep will be worked back and forth on two ndls.

With MC, CO 13 (15) sts and work back and forth in two-color garter st. On row 4 (WS) and on the following 4th row, increase 1 st at each side = 17 (19) sts.

After working in pattern for 2 (2³⁄₈) in / 5 (6) cm, bind off all sts.
Sew the instep to the foot, matching the center of the cast-on row of the shoe top with the center front of the brioche pattern, and join from marker to marker, along bound-off row and sides.

For the doubled top of the shoe, with MC, pick up and knit 28 (34) sts from the outside of the shoe to the heel, 7 (8) sts from the seamed side to the bound-off row, and 7 (8) sts from the bound-off side to the front = 42 (50) sts.
Work back and forth in stockinette for 1 in / 2.5 cm and then bind off all sts. Fold band and sew down, leaving front of "tube" open for cords.
Make a twisted cord about 21¾ in / 55 cm long with MC; fold it in half to twist together and then thread through folded band at ankle.

Make both shoes the same way.

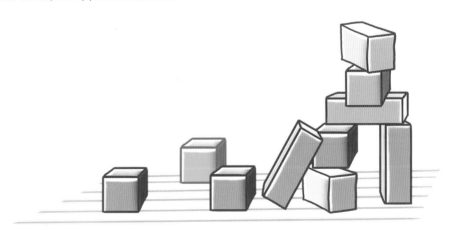

Everyone Needs a Flower

LEVE L OF DIFFICULTY
Easy

SIZE
0 – 3 months (approx)

(see page 127 for size measurements)

MATERIALS
Yarn: Schachenmayr Baby Wool (100% Merino wool, 25 g, 93 yds / 85 m) Orange (26), Green (70), Vanilla (22)

Needles: set of 4 or 5 dpn U.S. size 2.5 / 3 mm

Crochet hook: U.S. size C / 2.5 mm

GAUGE
28 sts and 36 rows in stockinette = 4 x 4 in / 10 x 10 cm.

Adjust needle size to obtain correct gauge.

STITCH PATTERNS

GARTER STITCH
Garter Stitch in the Round: Alternately knit 1 rnd, purl 1 rnd.
Garter Stitch worked back and forth:
Knit all rows.

RIBBING
K1, p1 around or across.

STRIPE SEQUENCE
* 2 rnds Orange, 2 rnds Vanilla, 2 rnds Green, 2 rnds Vanilla; rep from *.

INSTRUCTIONS

Begin on the sole with vanilla. Cast on 36 sts; divide sts evenly onto dpn and join, being careful not to twist cast-on row. Work around in garter st. On rnd 3 inc with M1: on ndls 1 and 4, inc after the first st on dpn; on ndls 2 and 4, inc before the last st on dpn. Increase the same way on every other round 3 more times = 52 sts. Now continue in garter stitch working in stripe sequence. After 18 rnds, work ribbing with orange as follows:
Rnd 1: 14 sts in ribbing, (k2tog) 12 times, 14 sts ribbing.
Rnd 2: Work around in ribbing.
Rnd 3: 14 sts in ribbing, (k2tog) 6 times, 14 sts in ribbing = 34 sts rem.

Work another 7 rounds in ribbing with orange and then continue in stripe pattern working back and forth, dividing sts at the center. Work 12 rows and then bind off with vanilla. Seam sole and weave in all tails on WS. At the top of the instep, sew on the little crocheted flower. Work 1 round of single crochet around the first round of orange on the sole.

LITTLE CROCHETED FLOWER
With Vanilla, (ch 3 and then sl st into first chain) 5 times. With Orange, make a French knot at the center of the flower.

Make both socks the same way.

For Beach Buddies

LEVEL OF DIFFICULTY
Easy

SIZE
0 – 6 months (approx)
(see page 127 for size measurements)

MATERIALS
Yarn: Schachenmayr Catania (100% cotton, 50 g, 137 yds / 125 m) Peacock (146)

Needles: set of 4 or 5 dpn U.S. size 2.5 / 3 mm

Extra needle for picking up sts

GAUGE
26 sts and 36 rows = 4 x 4 in / 10 x 10 cm.

Adjust needle size to obtain correct gauge.

STITCH PATTERNS

STOCKINETTE
Stockinette in the round: Knit all rows.
Stockinette back and forth: Knit on RS and purl on WS.

LACE WORKED IN THE ROUND
Rnd 1: * Yo, k2tog; rep from * around.
Rnd 2: Knit around.
Rnd 3: * K2tog, yo; rep from * around.
Rnd 4: Knit around.
Repeat these 4 rounds.

Lace worked back and forth.
Work as above for but purl across WS rows.

INSTRUCTIONS

CO 32 sts and divide evenly onto dpn; join, being careful not to twist cast-on row. Knit 3 rnds. On the next rnd, (k2tog, yo) around. Knit another 3 rnds; on rnd 1 make sure you knit all the yarn-overs on the lace rnd. Using an extra needle, pick up 32 sts on the cast-on row. Place picked up sts behind live sts and join the two sets by knitting the first st on front ndl together with first st on back needle around. Now work around in lace and stockinette: K10, 12 sts lace, k10. Work in pattern for 12 rounds and then work 4 rnds as (k1, p1) 5 times, 12 sts lace, (k1, p1) 5 times. Now work back and forth only over the 12 lace sts of instep for 1½ in / 4 cm. Pick up and knit 10 sts along the left side of the instep flap, k20, pick up and knit 10 sts along right side of instep and k12. Continue stockinette in the round for 9 rnds, and then purl 1 rnd. The sole is worked in stocki-nette. Dec with k2tog at beg of ndls 1 and 3 and the end of ndls 2 and 4. Repeat the dec rnd 4 times on every other rnd. Join the two halves of the sole with Kitchener st and then weave in all tails on WS.

Make the other sock the same way.

Off on a Big Trip

LEVEL OF DIFFICULTY
Intermediate

SIZE
0 – 6 months (approx)

(see page 127 for size measurements)

MATERIALS
Yarn: Schachenmayr Baby Wool (100% Merino wool, 25 g, 93 yds / 85 m) Navy blue (50), White (01), Red (30)

Needles: set of 4 or 5 dpn U.S. size 2.5 / 3 mm

Crochet hook U.S. size D-3 / 3 mm

GAUGE
28 sts and 36 rows in stockinette = 4 x 4 in / 10 x 10 cm.

Adjust needle size to obtain correct gauge.

STITCH PATTERNS

GARTER STITCH
Garter Stitch in the Round: Alternately knit 1 rnd, purl 1 rnd.
Garter Stitch back and forth: Knit all rows.

STOCKINETTE
Knit on RS and purl on WS.

STRIPE SEQUENCE 1
2 rnds Navy, 2 rnds White.

STRIPE SEQUENCE 2
2 rnds Navy, 2 rnds Red.

INSTRUCTIONS

With navy, cast on 36 sts and divide sts evenly over dpn; join, being careful not to twist cast-on row. Work stripe sequence 1 in garter stitch 6 times. Next work 2 rnds in navy and then make a lace row for the ties: *k2tog, yo; rep from * around. On the following rnd, knit, including all the yarnovers and then purl 1 rnd. On the next rnd, k12 with navy and then work the next 12 sts for the instep in stockinette and stripe sequence 2. Work back and forth over the 12 instep sts, repeating stripe pattern 6 times and ending with 1 row navy. Pick up and knit 10 sts along the side of the instep, k24, and then pick up and knit 10 sts on the other side of the instep, k12. Continue around in garter stitch: 2 rnds navy, 2 rnds white, 6 rnds Navy, 2 rnds white, 2 rnds navy, 2 rnds red.
Knit the sole back and forth with red only over the front 12 sts. At the end of the needle always knit the last st together with the first st on the side.
Continue until 12 sts remain and then join these 12 sts with the 12 sts on sole with Kitchener st (see page 122).
Weave in all tails on WS. For the tie cords, with red and crochet hook ch 90 and end off. Thread cord through lace row at ankle. Secure the cord ends with an overhand knot.

Make the other shoe the same way.

For Princesses

LEVEL OF DIFFICULTY
Intermediate

SIZES
0-3 months (approx)

3 (3¼, 3¾) in / 7.5 (8.5, 9.5) cm

The instructions for the first size are given before the parentheses; those for the second and third sizes are in order within parentheses. If only one number is given, it applies to all sizes.

MATERIALS
Yarn: Schachenmayr Baby Wool (100% Merino wool, 25 g, 93 yds / 85 m) White (01) and Pink (34) (or small amount pink)

Needles: set of 5 dpn U.S. sizes 1.5 – 4 / 2.5 – 3.5 mm

GAUGE
Pattern and stockinette

28 sts and 36 rnds = 4 x 4 in / 10 x 10 cm.

Adjust needle size to obtain correct gauge.

STITCH PATTERNS

STOCKINETTE
Worked back and forth: Knit on RS and purl on WS.
In the round: Knit all rounds.

PATTERN
Multiple of 4 sts.
Rnd 1: * P1, yo, sl 1-k1-psso, p1; rep from * around.
Rnd 2: * P1, k2tog (yarnover and following st), yo, p1; rep from * around.
Rnd 3: * P1, yo, sl 1-k1-psso, p1; rep from * around.
Repeat these 3 rounds.

INSTRUCTIONS

Begin with the pink ruffle. CO 84 (96, 108) sts and divide over dpn = 21 (24, 27) sts per ndl; join, being careful not to twist cast-on row. Knit 2 rnds. Change to white and decrease in the next rnd as follows: * Sl 2 knitwise at the same time, k1, pass slipped sts over knit st; rep from * around = 28 (32, 36) sts rem. Knit 1 rnd and then work pattern.
After working in pattern for 1¾ in / 4.5 cm, shape the foot. Work the short row heel (see page 118) over the sts on ndls 1 and 4. After completing heel, continue with pattern over ndls 2 and 3 and stockinette on ndls 1 and 4 to the toe. Work toe in stockinette with band shaping.

Make both socks alike.

Colorful Clowns

LEVEL OF DIFFICULTY
Easy

SIZE
3-6 months (approx)
(see page 127 for size measurements)

MATERIALS
Yarn: Schachenmayr Wash+Felt It! (100% wool, 50 g, 54 yds / 49 m) White (102)

Regia Softy Color 50 g Pastel (475)

Needles: set of 5 dpn US sizes 4 and 11 / 3.5 and 8 mm

GAUGE
16 sts and 22 rows in stockinette = 4 x 4 in / 10 x 10 cm.

24 sts and 36 rows after felting = 4 x 4 in / 10 x 10 cm.

Adjust needle sizes to obtain correct gauge.

Stockinette: Worked back and forth: Knit on RS and purl on WS.
In the round: Knit all rounds.

Reverse stockinette: Purl on all RS rows and knit on WS rows.

K2, p2

With two of the larger dpn and white, cast on 15 sts. Work back and forth in stockinette for 14 rows. On the next row, work to the center st, CO 1 st. The center front st is now the beginning of the round. Divide sts evenly onto 4 dpn (=4 sts per ndl) and join. With white, work in stockinette for 12 rnds and then shape toe.
Toe shaping: knit the first 2 sts on each ndl together until only 2 sts rem on each ndl. Cut yarn and pull tail through rem 8 sts; weave in tail on WS. Seam back of leg. With smaller dpn and pastel, pick up and knit 32 sts around top of leg. Knit 1 rnd and then work in ribbing for 4 in / 10 cm. BO in ribbing.

Make the second shoe the same way.

Wash shoes at 104°F / 40°C (see page 125) and pull into shape.

To make the bowties, use smaller ndls and CO 10 sts with pastel. Work 4 rows in stitch pattern 2 (reverse stockinette), then 5 rows in pattern 1 (stockinette), followed by 4 rows reverse stockinette. BO all sts. Secure bowties to top of foot as shown in photo.

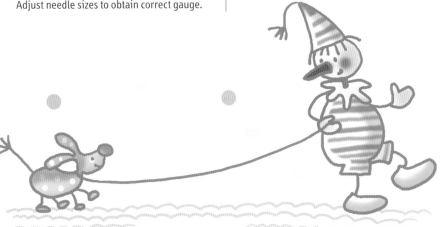

For the Cuddly Bunny

LEVEL OF DIFFICULTY
Easy

SIZE
Newborn (approx)

(see page 127 for size measurements)

MATERIALS
Yarn: Schachenmayr Ecological (100% wool, 50 g, 87 yds / 80 m) Exotic (1729) or Tundra (1725)

Regia Softy 50 g Tangerine (436) or Natural white (425)

Needles: set of 5 dpn US sizes 4 and 10 / 3.5 and 6 mm

GAUGE
16 sts and 22 rows in stockinette = 4 x 4 in / 10 x 10 cm

24 sts and 36 rows when felted = 4 x 4 in / 10 x 10 cm.

Adjust needle size to obtain correct gauge.

STITCH PATTERNS

STOCKINETTE
Worked back and forth: Knit on RS and purl on WS.
In the round: Knit all rounds.

RIBBING
K2, p2

INSTRUCTIONS

With two of the larger dpn and Ecological yarn, cast on 24 sts and work back and forth in stockinette for 22 rows. On the next row, knit to the center 2 sts and then divide sts over 4 dpn. The center front is now the beginning of the round. Join and knit 14 rnds and then shape toe.
Toe shaping: knit the first 2 sts on each ndl tog until only 2 sts rem on each dpn. Cut yarn and bring tail through rem 8 sts. Weave in tail on WS. Seam back of leg.
With smaller dpn and Softy, pick up and knit 32 sts around the top of the foot. Knit 1 rnd and then work in ribbing for 25 rnds. BO in ribbing.

Make the other sock the same way.

FELTING
Wash socks at 104°F / 40°C (see page 125) and pull into shape.

Little Flower Garden

LEVEL OF DIFFICULTY
Intermediate

SIZE
0 – 3 months (approx)

(see page 127 for size measurements)

MATERIALS
Yarn: Schachenmayr Extra Merino 100% Merino wool, 50 g, 138 yds / 126 m) White (01)

Regia Softy (61% polyamide/39% new wool, 50 g, 137 yds / 125 m) Fern (434)

Small amounts of 5 different colors wool yarn

Needles: set of 5 dpn US sizes 4-6 / 3.5-4 mm

Tapestry needle

GAUGE
22 sts and 30 rows in stockinette = 4 x 4 in / 10 x 10 cm.

Adjust needle size to obtain correct gauge

STITCH PATTERNS

STOCKINETTE
Worked back and forth: Knit on RS and purl on WS.
In the round: Knit all rounds.

GARTER STITCH
Worked back and forth: Knit all rows.

INSTRUCTIONS

With Softy fern, cast on 32 sts and divide evenly onto 4 dpn; join, being careful not to twist cast-on row. Knit 8 rnds. Change to white and work around in stockinette for 1½ in / 4 cm. Knit 11 and then work only on the next 10 sts for the instep for 1½ in / 4 cm. Pick up and knit 9 sts along side of instep, k22, pick up and knit 9 sts along other side of instep and then k10. Continue in stockinette for 10 rnds.

Now divide sts so there are 15 sts for each side of the sole and 10 sts at center front for instep. Work in garter st, always knitting together the last st with the first st of the side together. Continue until 10 sts rem. Join the sole with Kitchener st (see page 122). Cut yarn and weave in tail on WS. Decorate the socks with flowers embroidered in Daisy st (see page 126).

Make the other sock the same way.

Little Moon Princess

LEVEL OF DIFFICULTY
Experienced

SIZE
0 – 6 months (approx)
(see page 127 for size measurements)

MATERIALS
Yarn: Schachenmayr Baby Wool (100%
Merino wool, 25 g, 93 yds / 85 m) White (01)

Anchor Artiste metallic Fine (80% viscose/
20% metalized polyester, 25 g, 109 yds /
100 m) Silver (301)

Needles: set of 5 dpn US size 2.5 / 3 mm

Crochet hook: US size C-2 / 3 mm

GAUGE
28 sts and 36 rows in stockinette = 4 x 4 in /
10 x 10 cm.

Adjust needle size to obtain correct gauge.

STITCH PATTERNS

GARTER STITCH
Garter Stitch worked back and forth: Knit all sts.
Garter Stitch in the round: Alternately knit 1 rnd
and purl 1 rnd.

TWO-COLOR FISHERMAN'S RIB
Rnd 1 (holding silver and white together): * K1,
p1; rep from * around.
Rnd 2 (with white only): * K1 into stitch below,
p1; rep from * around.
Repeat rnds 1 and 2.

INSTRUCTIONS

Begin on the sole with white Baby Wool. Cast on
32 sts and divide sts evenly onto 4 dpn; join,
being careful not to twist cast-on row.
Work around in garter st. On the 3rd rnd, M1
after the first st on ndls 1 and 3 and before the
last st on ndls 2 and 4. Repeat the increases on
every other round another 3 times = 48 sts.
Next work 20 rnds in two-color fisherman's rib
and then continue in garter st as follows:
Rnd 1 (with white): K12, (k2tog) 12 times, k12 =
36 sts white.
Rnd 2: Purl.
Rnd 3 (with 2 strands silver): K12, (k2tog) 6
times, k12.
Rnd 4 (with 2 strands silver): Purl.
Rnd 5 (white): Knit.
Rnd 6 (white): Purl.
Continue in garter st with white and BO the 2
center front sts. Now work back and forth. Knit 2
rows and then make a lace row: (k2tog, yo)
across. On the following row knit all sts. Knit 10
rows with white. With 2 strands of silver held
together, pick up and knit 5 sts along each front
edge and knit 2 rows across all sts; BO.
Seam center of sole and then weave in all ends
on WS. Crochet a cord with white: ch 80 and
secure end through last ch. Thread cord through
lace row at ankle and tie a little knot at each end
of cord.

Make the other sock the same way.

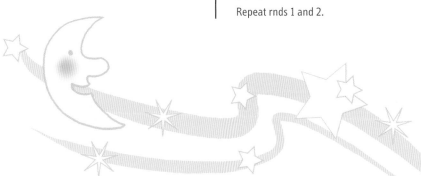

Please My Heart!

LEVEL OF DIFFICULTY
Experienced

SIZES
3 – 6 months (approx)

(see page 127 for size measurements)

MATERIALS
Yarn: Regia 4-ply (75% wool/25% polyamide, 50 g, 230 yds / 210 m) Pine (327)

Schachenmayr Baby Wool (100% Merino wool, 25 g, 93 yds / 85 m) Red (30) and White (01)

Needles: set of 5 dpn US size 2.5 / 3 mm

Crochet hook: US size B-1 / 2.5 mm

Tapestry needle

GAUGE
28 sts and 36 rows in stockinette = 4 x 4 in / 10 x 10 cm.

Adjust needle size to obtain correct gauge.

STITCH PATTERNS

GARTER STITCH
Garter Stitch worked back and forth: Knit all sts.
Garter Stitch in the round: Alternately knit 1 rnd and purl 1 rnd.

STOCKINETTE
Worked back and forth: Knit on RS and purl on WS.
In the round: Knit all rounds.

RIBBING
(K1, p1) across/around.

HALF FISHERMAN'S RIB IN THE ROUND
Rnd 1: * K1, p1; rep from * around.
Rnd 2: * K1 into stitch below, p1; rep from * around.
Repeat rnds 1 and 2.

CROCHETED CRAB STITCH
See page 124.

INSTRUCTIONS

Begin on the sole with red Baby Wool. Cast on 32 sts and divide sts evenly onto 4 dpn; join, being careful not to twist cast-on row. Work around in garter st. Increase on every other rnd as follows: M1 after the first st on ndls 1 and 3 and before the last st on ndls 2 and 4. Increase the same way on every other rnd 5 more times = 56 sts. Change to Regia pine and work in half-fisherman's rib for 14 rnds. Now work 23 sts and, with white, work in stockinette over the next 10 sts for the instep: k9 and then ssk with 1 white and 1 pine st from the side; turn, p9, p 1 white and 1 pine st tog tbl. Continue the same way, joining instep and side sts until 16 sts rem. Divide the sts over 4 dpn: 10 sts for the front, 11 for the side, 10 for the back, and 11 sts for the other side. With pine, work in ribbing for 6 rnds and then work 20 rnds in half-fisherman's rib, be aware that the inside of the cuff will be the side that shows. Work 1 rnd white and 1 rnd red in ribbing. BO with red as follows: K2tog , *put new st back on left ndl, k2tog; rep from * around. Seam the sole. Crochet around the instep with 1 rnd crab st in red and then embroider a little red heart with duplicate st (see page 122). Weave in all yarn ends neatly on WS.

Make the other shoe the same way.

Warm Feet from the Very Beginning

SOCKS, SOCKS...

When small children begin crawling and eventually walking, they need warm feet more than ever. With these soft, cozy socks, moving around is a lot more fun. Bright colors and motifs as well as interesting textures and embellishments give these designs flair/style/zing and are great fun to knit!

Colorful Stripes

LEVEL OF DIFFICULTY
Easy

SIZES
3-6 months (approx)

Foot length approx 3¼ (4) in / 8 (10) cm

The instructions for the 3¼ / 8 cm foot are given before the parentheses; those for the 4 in / 10 cm length are within parentheses. If only one number is given, it applies to both sizes.

MATERIALS
Yarn: Schachenmayr Baby Wool (100% Merino wool, 25 g, 93 yds / 85 m)

	Color 1	Color 2
Model A:	pink (35)	orange (26)
Model B:	green (70)	light blue (52)
Model C:	red (30)	orange (26)
Model D:	navy blue (50)	denim (51)

Needles: set of 4 or 5 dpn U.S. size 1.5-4 / 2.5-3.5 mm

GAUGE
28 sts and 36 rows in stockinette = 4 x 4 in / 10 x 10 cm.

28 sts and 50 rows in garter st = 4 x 4 in / 10 x 10 cm.

Adjust needle size to obtain correct gauge.

STITCH PATTERNS

RIBBING
(K1, p1) across/around.

GARTER STITCH
Garter Stitch worked back and forth: Knit all sts. Garter Stitch in the round: Alternately knit 1 rnd and purl 1 rnd.

STOCKINETTE
In the round: Knit all rounds.

INSTRUCTIONS

Begin with the sole. With smooth waste yarn, provisionally CO 36 (40) sts. Divide sts evenly over 4 dpn [9 (10) sts per dpn] and join, being careful not to twist cast-on row. With color 1, work around in garter st; beg of rnd = center of heel. Purl the first rnd. On the following rnd and the next 4 alternate rnds, increase 4 sts per rnd. On ndls 1 and 3, inc 1 st with M1 after the first st and, on ndls 2 and 4, M1 before the last st on ndl = 40 (44) sts after the first increase rnd and 56 (60) sts when rnd 10 is complete.

Work another 11 (13) rnds. Mark placement of the instep: mark the 22nd (23rd) st and the 35th (38th) st. On the next rnd (knit rnd), k34 (37) sts = 1 st before the 2nd marker, knit together the 2 sts before/after marker. Turn and continue in

garter st on the sts between the markers = 14 (16) sts. Now work back and forth only on instep sts.

On the next row RS, knit 13 (15) sts = 1 st before marker and knit marked st together with the following st; turn. Knit across 13 (15) sts and knit the marked st together with the following st; turn. Rep these short rows 9 (10) times = 20 (22) sts decreased and 36 (38) sts rem on the last row. Do not turn after the final decrease but knit the next 11 (12) sts to the rounded section where foot ends.

Work the leg in stockinette, alternating 2 rnds color 2 and 2 rnds color 1. On every other round, increase at the back of the leg with M1 after the 1st on ndl 1 and before the last st on ndl 4 a total of 2 times = 40 (42) sts. When leg is 3¼ in / 8.5 cm long (30 rnds), on the 8th stripe of color 2, work 6 rnds in k1/p1 ribbing with color 1 and then BO in ribbing.

Remove the waste yarn from the cast-on for sole, beginning where the tail hangs at the center of the heel, and divide the sts with the first 18 (20) on ndl 1 and the next 18 (20) sts on ndl 2. With ndls held parallel, seam the sole with Kitchener st (see page 122). Turn sock right side out.

Make both socks alike.

...Colorful Stripes

Little Ray
of Sunshine

Instructions page 50

Little Ray of Sunshine

LEVEL OF DIFFICULTY
Easy

SIZE
3-6 months (approx)

(see page 127 for size measurements)

MATERIALS
Yarn: Regia 4-ply (75% wool/25% polyamide, 50 g, 230 yds / 210 m) white (2080)
and small amount light blue (1945) or yellow
(2041)

Needles: set of 5 dpn U.S. size 0-2.5 / 2-3 mm

GAUGE
28 sts and 36 rows in stockinette = 4 x 4 in /
10 x 10 cm.

Adjust needle size to obtain correct gauge.

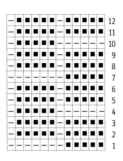

☐ = Knit 1
■ = Purl 1

STITCH PATTERNS

Ribbing: (K2tbl, p1) around.

STOCKINETTE

Worked back and forth: Knit on RS and purl
on WS.

In the round: Knit all rounds.

INSTRUCTIONS

With light blue, CO 36 sts, divide sts evenly over
dpn and join, being careful not to twist cast-on
row. Work 8 rnds in k2tbl/p1 ribbing.
Change to white and knit 1 rnd and then work 25
rnds in charted pattern for the leg. Change to
light blue and work Dutch heel following instructions on page 119. When turning the heel, work
10 rows with 6/6/6 sts. After completing heel,
change back to white and continue in charted
pattern over the instep and stockinette on the
sole. Shape the gusset on every other round until
36 sts rem.
After working 24 rnds, change to light blue and
work a band toe (see page 121). Turn sock inside
out and divide sts evenly over 2 ndls. With RS
facing RS, BO with three-needle bind-off.

As an alternative, knit the socks only with yellow.

Weave in all tails neatly on WS. Make both socks
alike.

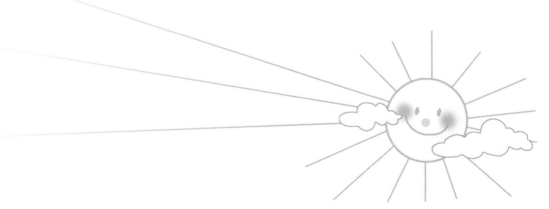

Fire Engine Red

LEVEL OF DIFFICULTY
Easy

SIZES
0-3 months (approx)

3 (3¼, 3¾) in / 7.5 (8.5, 9.5) cm

The instructions for the first size are given before the parentheses; those for the second and third sizes are in order within the parentheses. If only one number is given, it applies to all sizes.

MATERIALS
Yarn: Regia 4-ply (75% wool/25% polyamide, 50 g, 230 yds / 210 m) fire-engine red (2054) and yellow (2041); small amounts of orange (1259) and fern (1092)

Needles: set of 5 dpn U.S. size 0-2.5 / 2-3 mm

Crochet hook: US B/C / 2.5 mm

Blunt tapestry needle

GAUGE
30 sts and 42 rows in stockinette = 4 x 4 in / 10 x 10 cm.

Adjust needle size to obtain correct gauge.

STITCH PATTERNS
Ribbing: (K1, p1) around.

STOCKINETTE
Worked back and forth: Knit on RS and purl on WS.

In the round: Knit all rounds.

EMBROIDERED PLAID
Knit 6 rnds yellow, 1 rnd red, 3 rnds yellow, 1 rnd orange, 6 rnds yellow = total of 17 rnds.

INSTRUCTIONS

With yellow, CO 27 (31, 35) sts and divide sts over dpn; join, being careful not to twist cast-on row. Work 2 rnds k1, p1 ribbing and then the 17-round plaid sequence. Continue in stockinette with red only. On the first red rnd, dec with k2tog 3 times evenly spaced around = 24 (28, 32) sts. When leg is total of 2½ (3, 3) in / 6.5 (7.5, 7.5) cm long, work the foot with red.

Embroider the plaid stripes with chain st (see page 126), working in chain st between two knit sts. At the back, centered between the 1st and last sts, chain st with fern and then, moving clockwise, skip 1 (3, 5) sts and chain st with red, *move over 3 sts and chain st with orange, over 8 sts and chain st with red; rep from * once more and finish 3 sts over with chain st in orange.

At the top of the leg, make a crochet picot edging (see page 124). Join fern to cast-on row with 1 sl st, *ch 3 and then 1 sc into 1st ch, skip 1 st, sc 1; rep from * around and end with 1 sl st into the first sl st.

Make both socks alike.

Quick Take-off for Little Pilots

LEVEL OF DIFFICULTY
Intermediate

SIZE
6-9 months (approx)
(see page 127 for size measurements)

MATERIALS
Yarn: Regia 4-ply (75% wool/25% polyamide, 50 g, 230 yds / 210 m) denim (1932)

Needles: set of 5 dpn U.S. size 0-2.5 / 2-3 mm

Cable needle

GAUGE
28 sts and 36 rows in stockinette = 4 x 4 in / 10 x 10 cm.

Adjust needle size to obtain correct gauge.

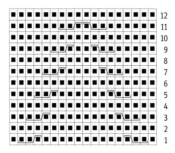

■ = Knit 1

■■/■ = Place 1 st onto cable needle and hold behind work; k2 and then k1 from cable ndl.

■■■ = Place 2 sts onto cable ndl and hold in front of work; k1 and then k2 from cable ndl.

STITCH PATTERNS

PICOT EDGING
Knit 4 rnds and then work 1 rnd (k2tog, yo) around. Knit 5 rnds. On the next rnd, pick up each st on cast-on row. Holding cast-on row sts behind set of live sts, join with the two sets of sts by knitting together the first st from each set. The fold at the lace row makes a picot or "mouse tooth" edging.

STOCKINETTE
Worked back and forth: Knit on RS and purl on WS.
In the round: Knit all rounds.

INSTRUCTIONS

CO 36 sts, divide over dpn and join, being careful not to twist cast-on row. Work the picot edging and then continue in charted pattern.
Work Rnds 1-12 and then Rnds 3-12, ending with Rnds 3-5.
After the final Rnd 5, work the Dutch heel (see page 119) over the sts on ndls 3 and 4 (= 18 sts). Work 14 rows for heel turning with 6/6/6 sts. Continue in charted pattern (beg on Rnd 6) on the instep and stockinette on the sole (see A Closer Look Below). Decrease for gusset on every other rnd until 36 sts rem.

A CLOSER LOOK
After the heel, work the instep as follows:
Rnds 6-12 once and then Rnds 3-12 twice.

Finish the foot with a band toe (see page 121). Turn sock inside out and divide sts evenly over 2 ndls. With RS facing RS, BO with three-needle bind-off.

Weave in all tails neatly on WS. Make both socks alike.

Ship Ahoy!

Instructions page 59

Ship Ahoy!

LEVEL OF DIFFICULTY
Easy

SIZES
3-6 & 6-9 months (approx)

(see page 127 for size measurements)

The instructions for size 13-15 are given before the parentheses; those for size 16-18 are within the parentheses. If only one number is given, it applies to both sizes.

MATERIALS
Yarn: Regia 4-ply (75% wool/25% polyamide, 50 g, 230 yds / 210 m) superwhite (2080) and navy (324)

Regia 4-ply (75% wool/25% polyamide, 50 g, 230 yds / 210 m) small amounts fire-engine red (2054) or yellow (2041)

Needles: set of 5 dpn U.S. size 0-2.5 / 2-3 mm

GAUGE
30 sts and 42 rows in stockinette = 4 x 4 in / 10 x 10 cm.

Adjust needle size to obtain correct gauge.

STITCH PATTERNS

RIBBING
(K1, p1) around.

STOCKINETTE
Worked back and forth: Knit on RS and purl on WS.
In the round: Knit all rounds.

STRIPE SEQUENCE
Alternate 4 Rnds white, 4 Rnds navy.

INSTRUCTIONS

With navy, CO 40 (44) sts and divide sts evenly over dpn; join, being careful not to twist cast-on row. Work in k1/p1 ribbing for 1½ in / 4 cm. Beg of the rnd is center back. Continue around in stockinette, working 28 rnds in stripe sequence. Place sts on ndls 2 and 3 on a holder and work the heel over the sts on ndls 1 and 4 and. With red or yellow, work the Short row heel (see page 118). After completing heel, work in stripe pattern for 3¼ (4) in / 8.5 (10) cm (as measured from center of heel) and then, with red or yellow, work the band toe. Shape toe as follows: Ndls 1 and 3: Knit across until 3 sts rem and then k2tog, k1. Ndls 2 and 4: K1, ssk, knit rem sts across. Decrease on every other rnd 3 (4) times and then on every rnd 4 times.

Cut yarn and pull tail through remaining 8 sts. Weave in all yarn tails neatly on WS.

Make the other sock the same way.

Little Ladybug

LEVEL OF DIFFICULTY
Intermediate

SIZE
12-18 months (approx)

(see page 127 for size measurements)

MATERIALS
Yarn: Regia 4-ply Mineral Colors (75% wool, 25% polyamide, 50 g, 230 yds / 210 m) aragonite (4377) and black (2066)

Needles: set of 5 dpn U.S. size 0-2.5 / 2-3 mm

GAUGE
28 sts and 36 rows in stockinette = 4 x 4 in / 10 x 10 cm.

Adjust needle size to obtain correct gauge.

STITCH PATTERNS

RIBBING
(K2, p1) around.

STOCKINETTE
Worked back and forth: Knit on RS and purl on WS.
In the round: Knit all rounds.

INSTRUCTIONS

With aragonite, CO 36 sts and divide sts evenly on dpn; join, being careful not to twist cast-on row. Work 8 rnds k2/p1 ribbing and then knit 1 rnd. Next, work pattern as follows:

Note: Do not cut color not in use; carry unused colors up on WS. When changing colors, twist the two strands around each other on WS to avoid holes.

Rnd 1, with black: (Sl 2 purlwise, k2) around.
Rnd 2, with red: (K2, sl 2 purlwise) around.
After completing 21 rnds of stripe pattern, work in stockinette as follows:
(1 rnd black, 1 rnd aragonite) 2 times.
(2 rnds black, 2 rnds aragonite) 2 times.

Now, with aragonite, work the Dutch heel (see page 118) over the sts on ndls 3 and 4. For heel turning, work 12 rows with 6/6/6 sts. After completing heel, work in the color sequence below and, at the same time, shape gusset on every other rnd until 36 sts rem.
3 rnds black, 3 rnds aragonite, 3 rnds black, 3 rnds aragonite, 3 rnds black, 3 rnds aragonite, 4 rnds black, 4 rnds aragonite, 4 rnds black, 1 rnd aragonite.
Finish with a band toe in aragonite (see page 121). Turn sock inside out and divide sts evenly over 2 ndls. BO with three-needle bind-off.

Weave in all tails neatly on WS. Make both socks alike.

Purple Pinwheel

LEVEL OF DIFFICULTY
Easy

SIZE
6-12 months (approx)

(see page 127 for size measurements)

MATERIALS
Yarn: Regia 4-ply (75% wool/25% polyamide, 50 g, 230 yds / 210 m) cardinal red (1078)

Schachenmayr Extra Merino (100% Merino wool, 50 g, 138 yds / 126 m) cyclamen (32)

Needles: set of 5 dpn U.S. size 0-2.5 / 2-3 mm

GAUGE
28 sts and 36 rows in stockinette with Regia = 4 x 4 in / 10 x 10 cm.

Adjust needle size to obtain correct gauge.

STITCH PATTERNS

RIBBING
(K2tbl, p1) around.

STOCKINETTE
Worked back and forth: Knit on RS and purl on WS.
In the round: Knit all rounds.

INCREASE ROUNDS
K1f&b into every st around. Knit into stitch but leave st on left needle; knit into back of same st and then slip sts off ndl.

DECREASE ROUNDS
K2tog around.

INSTRUCTIONS

With cardinal red, CO 36 sts and divide evenly over dpn; join, being careful not to twist cast-on row. Work 4 rnds ribbing.
*With cyclamen, work an increase round and then 4 rnds stockinette. With cardinal, work a decrease round and then 4 rnds stockinette. Rep from * once more.
Now, with cardinal, work 4 rnds ribbing. With cardinal, work the Dutch heel (see page 119) over 18 sts. Continue with the instep worked in ribbing and the sole in stockinette; decreasing for gusset on every other rnd until 36 sts rem.

After completing 26 rnds, work the band toe (see page 121). Turn sock inside out and divide sts evenly over 2 ndls. BO with three-needle bind-off.

Weave in all tails neatly on WS. Make both socks alike.

This pattern can be worked with any stitch count you like!

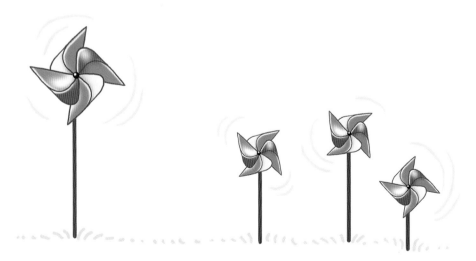

Hippity Hoppity Horse

LEVEL OF DIFFICULTY
Experienced

SIZE
6-12 months (approx)

(see page 127 for size measurements)

MATERIALS
Yarn: Regia 4-ply (75% wool/25% polyamide, 50 g, 230 yds / 210 m) natural (1992)

Regia Hand-dyed Effect (70% superwash wool/25% polyamide/5% acrylic, 100 g, 459 yds / 420 m) aragonite (6557)

Needles: set of 5 dpn U.S.size 0-2.5 / 2-3 mm

GAUGE
28 sts and 36 rows in stockinette = 4 x 4 in / 10 x 10 cm.

Adjust needle size to obtain correct gauge.

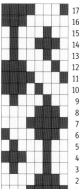

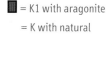

■ = K1 with aragonite

= K with natural

17 16 15 14 13 12 11 10 9 8 7 6 5 4 3 2 1

STITCH PATTERNS

STOCKINETTE
Worked back and forth: Knit on RS and purl on WS.

In the round: Knit all rounds.

INSTRUCTIONS

With natural, CO 40 sts and divide evenly over dpn; join, being careful not to twist cast-on row.
Rnd 1: (K1, p1) around.
Rnd 2 (aragonite): Knit all the knit sts with aragonite, slip all purl sts wyb.
Rnd 3 (natural): Slip all the knit sts wyb, purl all purl sts with natural.
Work all even-numbered rounds as for Rnd 2 and all odd-numbered rnds as for Rnd 3.
Repeat this sequence until there are 7 rnds worked with each color.
With natural, work 2 rnds in k1/p1 ribbing and then knit 2 rnds. Next work rows 1-17 of charted pattern. Twist yarns around each other every 2 sts to avoid long floats and holes in the knitting. After completing charted rows, knit 2 rnds with aragonite.
Work the Dutch heel over 20 sts (see page 119). For heel turning, work 16 rows of 6/8/6 sts. Shape gusset on every other round until 40 sts rem.
Work foot in the following color sequence:
6 rnds aragonite (from the heel), 2 rnds natural, 9 rnds aragonite, 2 rnds natural, 7 rnds aragonite, 2 rnds natural.
With aragonite, work the band toe (see page 121). Turn sock inside out and divide sts evenly over 2 ndls. BO with three-needle bind-off.

Weave in all tails neatly on WS. Make both socks alike.

The Winter King

LEVEL OF DIFFICULTY
Intermediate

SIZE
18-24 months (approx)

(see page 127 for size measurements)

MATERIALS
Yarn: Regia 4-ply (75% wool/25% polyamide, 50 g, 230 yds / 210 m) light blue (1945), lavender (1988), and royal (540)

Needles: set of 5 dpn U.S. size 1.5 / 2.5 mm

GAUGE
30 sts and 42 rows in stockinette = 4 x 4 in / 10 x 10 cm.

Adjust needle size to obtain correct gauge.

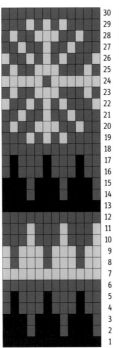

□ = K1 with light blue
■ = K1 with lavender
■ = K1 with royal

STITCH PATTERNS

STOCKINETTE
Worked back and forth: Knit on RS and purl on WS.
In the round: Knit all rounds.

RIBBING:
(K1, p1) around.

TWO-COLOR STRANDED KNITTING
See chart.

INSTRUCTIONS

With lavender, CO 48 sts and divide evenly on dpn; join, being careful not to twist cast-on row. Work in k1/p1 ribbing for 12 rnds and then knit 1 rnd. Continue in two-color stranded knitting following chart and then knit 8 rnds with lavender. With royal, work the Dutch heel (see page 119) over the sts on ndls 1 and 4. After turning the heel, with lavender, shape gusset by decreasing on ndls 1 and 4: ndl 1: knit until 3 sts rem, k2tog, k1; knit across ndls 2 and 3; ndl 4: k1, ssk, knit rem sts. Decrease on every other round until 48 sts rem. Continue in stockinette until sock is desired length to toe. With royal, decrease for a star toe (see page 121).

Make both socks alike.

Raspberries and Whipped Cream

LEVEL OF DIFFICULTY
Experienced

SIZE
12-18 months (approx)
(see page 127 for size measurements)

MATERIALS
Yarn: Regia 4-ply Color (75% wool, 25% polyamide, 50 g, 230 yds / 210 m) Fräulein (1804)

Regia 4-ply (75% wool, 25% polyamide, 50 g, 230 yds / 210 m) superwhite (2080)

Needles: set of 5 dpn U.S. size 1.5 / 2.5 mm

GAUGE
30 sts and 42 rows in stockinette = 4 x 4 in / 10 x 10 cm.

Adjust needle size to obtain correct gauge.

STITCH PATTERNS
Paving Stones (multiple of 4)
Rnd 1 (superwhite): Knit.
Rnds 2-5 (superwhite): Purl.
Rnd 6 (Fräulein): *K1, drop the next st and unravel down 4 rnds, with left ndl, pick up the stitch and the 4 loose strands and knit st and strands together, k2; rep from * around.
Rnd 7 (Fräulein): Knit.
Rnd 8 (superwhite): Knit.
Rnds 9-12 (superwhite): Purl.
Rnd 13 (Fräulein): *K3, drop the next st and unravel down 4 rnds, with left ndl, pick up the stitch and the 4 loose strands and knit st and strands together, rep from * around.
Rnd 14 (Fräulein): Knit.
Repeat Rnds 1-14.

STOCKINETTE
Worked back and forth: Knit on RS and purl on WS.
In the round: Knit all rounds.

INSTRUCTIONS

With Fräulein, CO 44 sts and divide evenly on dpn; join, being careful not to twist cast-on row. Begin by knitting 8 rnds for the rolled edge and then work in paving stones pattern for 21 rnds. Continue in paving stones pattern but only with Fräulein. When leg is about 4 ¾ in / 12 cm long and ending on a Row 6 or 13 of pattern, begin short row heel over sts on ndls 1 and 4 (see page 118).

After completing heel, work (with Fräulein only) in stockinette on ndls 1 and 4 for sole and in paving stones pattern on ndls 2 and 3 for instep. When foot is 4 in / 10.5 cm long, work star toe as follows: begin toe by knitting 1 rnd, decreasing to 40 sts with k2tog at beg of each ndl. Knit 2 rnds and then work star toe (see page 121).

Make the other sock the same way.

Surrounded by Angels

LEVEL OF DIFFICULTY
Intermediate

SIZE
2-3 yrs (approx)

(see page 127 for size measurements)

MATERIALS
Yarn: Regia 4-ply (75% wool, 25% polyamide, 50 g, 230 yds / 210 m)

Superwhite (2080)

Regia Softy (61% polyamide/39% new wool, 50 g, 137 yds / 125 m) natural (425)

Anchor Artiste Metallic (80% viscose, 20% metalized polyester, 25 g, 109 yds / 100 m) Gold (300)

Needles: 2 sets of 5 dpn U.S. size 0-2.5 / 2-3 mm

Embroidery needle

GAUGE
30 sts and 42 rows in stockinette = 4 x 4 in / 10 x 10 cm.

Adjust needle size to obtain correct gauge.

STITCH PATTERNS

RIBBING
(K2, p2) across/around.

STOCKINETTE
Worked back and forth: Knit on RS and purl on WS.
In the round: Knit all rounds.

SEED ST
Rnd 1: (K1, p1) around.
Rnd 2: (P1, k) around.

INSTRUCTIONS

To make the first ruffle, CO 96 sts with Softy natural and one set of dpn. Divide sts evenly on dpn and join, being careful not to twist cast-on row. Knit 8 rnds. On the next rnd, dec with k2tog around. Knit 4 more rounds, cut yarn and set piece aside.

For the second ruffle, CO 96 sts with Superwhite on the other set of dpn. Divide sts evenly on dpn and join, being careful not to twist cast-on row. Work 8 rnds in seed st. On the following rnd, dec with k2tog around. Knit 1 more rnd.

Place the first ruffle inside the second one and hold the two sets of needles parallel (the ruffled edges will also both be parallel). With superwhite, join the two sets of sts by knitting together the first st from each ndl. Continue with superwhite, working 10 rnds k2/p2 ribbing. Now work 32 rnds in stockinette for the leg and then make the short row heel (see page 118). Knit 43 rnds in stockinette for the foot; cut superwhite yarn. Join Softy natural and make a band toe (see page 121).

FINISHING
Weave in all yarn tails neatly on WS. Use the Artiste metallic yarn to embroider six-point stars (made with a cross bisected by a third line) evenly spaced around the leg, using stitch lines to guide you.

Make both socks alike.

Conquering the World

SLIPPERS AND HOUSE SOCKS

On their feet all day-this is how children explore the world. Now they are ready for slippers and socks with a bit more stability. Once again you have the choice: would you prefer a jungle sock entwined with a snake, socks with whimsical duck feet, perhaps strappy ballerina slippers, or washer-felted slippers with little bells? The slippers are protected with either a latex coating or a heavy felt sole. With this many charming socks and slippers to choose from only one thing is certain, you'll want to make several pairs.

For My Toys

LEVEL OF DIFFICULTY
Intermediate

SIZE
6-9 months (approx)

(see page 127 for size measurements)

MATERIALS
Yarn: Schachenmayr Wash+Felt-it! Fine (100% wool, 50 g, 109 yds / 100 m) violet (118)

Schachenmary Wash+Felt-it! multicolor fine (100% wool, 50 g, 109 yds / 100 m) Jamaica (1082)

Needles: circular and set of 5 dpn U.S. size 8 / 5 mm

2 flower buttons, 5/8 in / 1.5 cm diameter

GAUGE
16 sts and 22 rows in stockinette = 4 x 4 in / 10 x 10 cm.

After felting, 24 sts and 36 rows = 4 x 4 in / 10 x 10 cm.

Adjust needle size to obtain correct gauge.

STITCH PATTERN

STOCKINETTE
Work back and forth: Knit on RS and purl on WS.
In the round: Knit all rounds.

INSTRUCTIONS

For the right shoe, with violet and circular ndl, CO 42 sts and work back and forth in stockinette. On the 5th row, make buttonhole as follows: K 1, k2tog, yo twice, k2tog, k36, k1. On Row 6, knit the first yo and purl the second yo. At the end of Row 12, BO the last 6 sts and cut yarn. The rem 36 sts are worked in the round with Jamaica (4x9sts). Join, dividing sts evenly over dpn and continue in stockinette. The round begins at the center front. After 3 rnds, work only on 10 sts at center front (5 sts each from ndls 1 and 4). Work back and forth over these 10 sts for 20 rows for sole of foot. Return to knitting in the round, picking up and knitting 11 sts along each side of sole = 58 sts. Begin round at center front, work 10 rnds over all the sts, and then cut yarn. Finish the shoe with violet. Knit 1 rnd and then purl 1 rnd. Rearrange the sts so that the 10 center front sts are on one ndl, the 10 center back sts on another ndl and the 19 sts at each side are on separate ndls. Work back and forth only over the 10 center front sts while decreasing sts at the sides: From the center front, k4, *skp (sl 1, k1, psso); turn, sl 1, p8, p2tog; turn. Sl 1, k8; rep from * until all 19 sts at each side have been eliminated. Join the rem 2 sets of 10 sts with Kitchener st.

Make the left shoe to match, reversing shaping.

FELTING
Wash socks at 104°F / 40°C (see page 125) and pull into shape.

FINISHING
After felting shoes, sew on buttons.

GENERAL INFORMATION FOR THE FOLLOWING THREE PATTERNS

The slippers with short row patterns are for the experienced knitter who is up for a challenge. The pieces with elongated rows of radiating pattern (short rows)on the top of the foot require concentration while knitting and turning. Without the short rows, the knitting is much simpler and goes much more quickly. It is knit in three stages, but in one piece: the sole, the side of the foot and the back of the foot.

All three variations (pp76-85) each shoe can be worn on either foot.

TIPS AND TRICKS

• If you discover that you have either one more or less stitch than you should, it is easy to discreetly increase or decrease individual stitches.

• Soles begin at the toe and end at the heel.

• For a thicker sole, either double the yarn, or use a thicker yarn, but maintain the same needle size.

• If you cast on normally and knit with edge stitches, the stitches for the side of the foot must be picked up from the edge.

• To facilitate picking up the stitches around the edge of the sole, begin each row with a yarnover. Make sure these edge yarnovers remain on the needle, un-worked. Do not work these stitches on subsequent rows. After completing several rows, when picking up the edge yarnovers, use an extra needle so that the edge loops can sit on the outer needle and the stitches to be knit are on the central needle. Once the last sole row is completed, begin working in the round and picking up the edge loops. Stitches only need to be picked up from the cast on edge. It is easier with a circular needle.

• If using a circular needle, try the provisional/tubular cast on (see p 117) and wrap the yarn around the needle cable to create the edge yarnovers.

• In addition, the rows on the loops (=x2) are easy to count. The number of loops is the same as the number of stitches that you'll be knitting around on.

• If you're knitting on a circular needle, the foot-side stitches need to be held on a separate part of the needle as the foot-back stitches. After knitting the sole, you'll find your needle tips at the center of the heel. In order to continue knitting in the round, pull out a needle cable-loop at the center of the toe. Now you can continue as you would on two straight needles. When changing needles, the needle tip and a piece of the needle cable must be pulled out in such a way that before knitting on the other side of the round, a needle cable remains jutting out.

Arrange the stitches as you would for Magic Loop Method, search for "magic loop" on the internet if you are not familiar with this technique.

All My Clothes
are Green

Instructions pages 78-79

All My Clothes Are Green

LEVEL OF DIFFICULTY
Intermediate

SIZE
12 months (approx)

(see page 127 for size measurements)

MATERIALS
Yarn: Regia 4-ply (75% wool/25% polyamide, 50 g, 230 yds / 210 m) pine (327) = color 1 for the sole and Chinese lantern (1111) = color 3 for instep

Regia 4-ply, small amounts fern (1092) = color 2

Needles: set of 5 dpn or 48 in / 120 cm Magic loop circular U.S. size 1.5 / 2.5 mm

GAUGE
30 sts and 42 rnds in stockinette = 4 x 4 in / 10 x 10 cm.

Adjust needle size to obtain correct gauge.

STITCH PATTERNS

STOCKINETTE

Worked back and forth: Knit on RS and purl on WS.
In the round: Knit all rounds.

GARTER STITCH

Garter Stitch worked back and forth:
Knit all rows.
Garter Stitch in the round: Alternately knit 1 rnd and purl 1 rnd.

INSTRUCTIONS

SOLE

Color 1: work back and forth in garter st from the toe to the heel.
CO 4 sts with provisional cast on (see page 117).
Rows 1-9: On every other row, M1 after the first and before the last st of row = 14 sts.
Rows 10-29: Knit.
Row 30: Dec 1 st each at beg and end of row = 12 sts rem.
Rows 31-39: Knit.
Row 40: Dec 1 st each at beg and end of row = 10 sts rem.
Rows 41-59: Knit.
Row 60: Dec 1 st each at beg and end of row = 8 sts rem.
Row 61: Knit.
Row 62: Dec 1 st each at beg and end of row = 6 sts rem.
Row 63: K3 to center of heel. Pick up and knit sts

around the sole for a total of 72 sts.
Mark the center of heel and tip of toe. If working on a circular ndl, at the center of toe, pull out a ndl cable-loop so that you can continue knitting in the round in two separate sections. (Magic Loop method)

SIDE OF FOOT

Work in the round, beg at center back. Knit 1 rnd with color 1 = continue with the existing color. Purl 1 rnd with color 1, knit 4 rnds with color 2, knit 1 rnd with color 3. These rounds begin and end at center of toe.

INSTEP

Now work short rows in stockinette st. Mark center toe and heel, and on either side of each marker should be 24 sts, 48 total.
The 12 sts to the right and to the left of the heel marker (24 sts) are put on hold. The instep will be worked on the rem 24 sts (12 on either side of the toe marker). Beg at center of toe, k3; turn, yo, (see page 76). For this yarnover, wrap the yarn around the cable after the turn, at the beginning of the row. At the end of the row, this loop will always be knit together with the next stitch and 1 stitch will be increased (an increase of 2 sts in every row). On the RS, slip the yarnover, knit the next st and pass slipped st over. Continue with short row shaping until there are 16 sts on working needle (8 sts on either side of the center of toe).
Now from the existing 16 sts, work 15 sts, k3tog (16th st + yarnover + 1 st from holder).

On RS, work as follows: Sl 1 rem st + yarnover together, k 1 st from holder and pass over slipped sts.
Now work to place marked between the heel and instep. Beg working in the round again and, on every rnd, join the last st on holder with the first instep st and the last instep st with the next st on holder until 48 sts rem. Work 4 rnds in stockinette over these 48 sts to begin leg and then continue in k2/p2 ribbing until leg is desired length.

Make the other shoe the same way.

Bright, Brighter, Brightest

LEVEL OF DIFFICULTY
Intermediate

SIZE
3-6 months (approx)

(see page 127 for size measurements)

MATERIALS
Yarn: Regia 4-ply (75% wool/25% polyamide, 50 g, 230 yds / 210 m) Cardinal (1078) = color 1 for sole and Nordic mountain (5514) = color 3 for instep

Regia 4-ply, small amount Lavender (1988) = color 2 for sides of foot

Needles: set of 5 dpn or 48 in / 120 cm Magic loop circular U.S. size 1.5 / 2.5 mm

GAUGE
30 sts and 42 rounds in stockinette = 4 x 4 in / 10 x 10 cm

Adjust needle size to obtain correct gauge.

STITCH PATTERNS

STOCKINETTE
Worked back and forth: Knit on RS and purl on WS.
In the round: Knit all rounds.

GARTER STITCH
Garter Stitch worked back and forth:
Knit all rows.

INSTRUCTIONS

SOLE
With color 1, work back and forth in rows from the toe to the heel.
CO 4 sts with Italian cast-on (see page 117).
Rows 1-9: On every other row, M1 after the first and before the last st of row = 14 sts.
Rows 10-19: Knit.
Row 20: Dec 1 st each at beg and end of row = 12 sts rem.
Rows 21-29: Knit.
Row 30: Dec 1 st each at beg and end of row = 10 sts rem.
Rows 31-39: Knit.
Row 40: Dec 1 st each at beg and end of row = 8 sts rem.
Row 41: Knit.

... Bright, Brighter, Brightest

Row 42: Dec 1 st each at beg and end of row = 6 sts rem.

Row 43: K3 to center of heel. Pick up and knit sts around the sole for a total of 52 sts.

Mark the center of heel and tip of toe. If using a long circular ndl, pull out a loop of cable at the center of toe. You can now knit around with Magic Loop method.

SIDE OF FOOT

Work around, with beg of rnd at center back of heel. Knit 1 rnd with color 1 = continue with the previous color.

Purl 1 rnd with color 1, knit 4 rnds with color 2, knit 1 rnd with color 3. These rounds begin and end at center of toe.

INSTEP

Now work short rows in stockinette st. Mark center toe and heel, and on either side of each marker should be 24 sts, 48 total. The 12 sts to the right and to the left of the heel marker (24 sts) are put on hold. The instep will be worked on the rem 24 sts (12 on either side of the toe marker). Beg at center of toe, k3; turn, yo, (see page 76). For this yarnover, wrap the yarn around the cable after the turn, at the beginning of the row. At the end of the row, this loop will always be knit together with the next stitch and 1 stitch will be increased (an increase of 2 sts in every row). On the RS, slip the yarnover, knit the next st and pass slipped st over. Work the additional st. Continue with short row shaping until there are 12 sts on working needle (6 sts on either side of the center of toe).

Now from the existing 12 sts, work 11 sts, k3tog (12th st + yarnover + 1 st from holder).

On RS, work as follows: Sl last st, sl yarnover, k 1 st from holder and pass slipped sts over k st, turn, and again begin with a yo. Now work to place marked between the heel and instep. Beg working in rounds again and, on every rnd, join the last st on holder with the first instep st and the last instep st with the next st on holder until 40 sts rem. Work 4 rnds in stockinette over these 40 sts to begin leg and then continue in k2/p2 ribbing until leg is desired length.

Little Jumping Jacks

Instructions on pages 84-95

Little Snails

LEVEL OF DIFFICULTY
Intermediate

SIZE
3 – 6 months (approx)
(see page 127 for size measurements)

MATERIALS
Yarn: Schachenmayr Baby Soft (60% Acrylic/
40% nylon, 25 g, 77 yds / 70 m) pink (135)

Needles: set of 5 dpn U.S. size 2.5 / 3 mm

Notions: 2 small buttons

GAUGE
22 sts and 30 rows in stockinette = 4 x 4 in /
10 x 10 cm.

Adjust needle size to obtain correct gauge.

STITCH PATTERNS

GARTER STITCH

Garter Stitch worked back and forth: Knit all sts.
Garter Stitch in the round: Alternately knit 1 rnd
and purl 1 rnd.

LEAF PATTERN (MULTIPLE OF 6)

Rnd 1: *3-in-1 st = (k1, p1, k1) into 1 st, p3; rep
from * around.
Rnds 2-3: *K3, p3; rep from * around.
Rnd 4: *Sl 1-k2tog-psso, p1, 3-in-1, p1; rep from *
around.
Rnds 5-6: P2, *k3, p3; rep from * around; last rep
ends p1.
Repeat Rnds 1-6.

INSTRUCTIONS

Begin at the sole and CO 32 sts. Divide sts evenly
over dpn and join, being careful not to twist cast-
on row. Work around in garter st. On the 3rd rnd,
increase with M1 after the 1st on ndls 1 and 4
and before the last st on ndls 2 and 4. Rep the
increase 3 times on every other rnd = 48 sts.
Now work in leaf pattern for 14 rnds and then
continue in garter st:
Rnd 1: K12, (k2tog) 12 times, k12.
Rnd 2: Purl.
Rnd 3: K12, (k2tog) 6 times, k12.
Rnd 4: Purl.
Rnd 5: Knit.
Rnd 6: Purl.

For the right shoe, knit the first 8 sts, BO the next
14 sts, and then knit back and forth over rem 8
sts of ndl 4. At the end of next RS row, CO 14 sts
for strap. Continue in garter st, making buttonhole on 4th row with k2tog, yo. On the following
row, knit yarnover through back loop. After
completing 7 rows of strap, BO all sts. Seam
sole and weave in all yarn tails neatly on WS.
Sew on button.

Make left shoe to match (reversing placement
of strap).

For Ballerinas

LEVEL OF DIFFICULTY
Easy

SIZES
0-3 months (approx)

3¼ (3¾) in / 8.5 (9.5) cm

The instructions for the 3¼ in / 8.5 cm foot are given before the parentheses; those for the 3¾ in / 9.5 cm length are within parentheses. If only one number is given, it applies to both sizes.

MATERIALS
Yarn: Regia 4-ply (75% wool, 25% polyamide, 50 g, 230 yds / 210 m) Fräulein (1804)

Needles: U.S. size 0-2.5 / 2-3 mm

Crochet hook: U.S. size A-B / 2-2.5 mm

Notions: 2 buttons

GAUGE
30 sts and 42 rows = 4 x 4 in / 10 x 10 cm.

Adjust needle size to obtain correct gauge.

STITCH PATTERNS

GARTER STITCH
Garter Stitch worked back and forth: Knit all sts.

INSTRUCTIONS

RIGHT SANDAL
Begin with the sole. CO 40 (46) sts and work back and forth in garter st. Knit 1 row and then increase: K1, M1, k18 (21), M1, k2, M1, k18 (21), M1, k1 = 44 (50) sts. Rep this increase row on every other row 5 (6) times = 64 (74) sts. There will be 2 additional sts at center after each inc row and 18 (21) sts at each side. Knit 2 more rows to finish the sole.

Now knit 10 (12) rows over the 64 (74) sts. On the following row k22 (25) and then *k2tog, k2, k2tog, k2, k2tog*, k0 (4) at center front, and the rep * to * rep 1 time and rem k22 (25) = 59 (68) sts rem. On the next RS row, k22 (25), *k2tog, k2, k2tog*, k2 (6) and rep * to * 1 time, and knit rem sts = 54 (64) sts rem. On the following RS row, k22 (25), *k2tog, k2, from * rep 1 (2) times., k2tog, knit rem sts = 51 (60) sts.

For larger size only (foot length 3¾ in / 9.5 cm), on next RS row: k25, *k2tog, k2; rep from * 1 time, k2tog, knit rem sts = 57 sts. After a total of 18 (20) rows from the sole, k17 (19), BO center 17 (19) sts, and k17 (19) sts. Now knit 8 rows over the 17 (19) sts of right half, and then BO all sts. For the strap, CO 16 (18) sts and then knit across the 17 (19) of the left half = 33 (37) sts. Knit 8 rows over these 33 (37) sts, and, on the 4th row make a buttonhole in the strap. Knit the 3rd and 4th sts tog and yo; on the following row, knit the yarnover. After completing the 8 rows, BO all sts. Seam sole and back and sew on button. Work 1 round single crochet around the last ridge of the sole.

Make left sandal to match (reversing placement of strap).

Blackfoot Indians

LEVEL OF DIFFICULTY
Intermediate

SIZES
12-18 months (approx)

(see page 127 for size measurements)

MATERIALS
Yarn: Regia 4-ply (75% wool, 25% polyamide, 50 g, 230 yds / 210 m) Wave Color red (7550)

Needles: set of 5 dpn U.S. size 0-2.5 / 2-3 mm

Foot-shaped cookie cutter

Regia ABS-Latex, black

Small glass

Piece of paper

Piece of plastic wrap

GAUGE
28 sts and 36 rows in stockinette = 4 x 4 in / 10 x 10 cm.

Adjust needle size to obtain correct gauge.

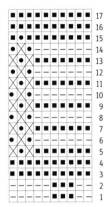

–	= Knit 1
■	= Purl 1
⊠	= Sl 1 st with 1 yarnover purlwise
•	= Knit 1 st with 1 yarnover together

STITCH PATTERNS

RIBBING
K1tbl, p1 around or across.

STOCKINETTE
Worked back and forth: Knit on RS and purl on WS.

In the round: Knit all rounds.

CHARTED PATTERN
Work every rnd as indicated on chart; repeat = Rnds 1-17.

INSTRUCTIONS

CO 40 sts and divide evenly over dpn; join, being careful not to twist cast-on row. Work 8 rnds in ribbing and then work 2 repeats of charted pattern. Next (3rd repeat), work only Rows 1-15 of chart. Work Dutch heel over sts on ndls 1 and 4 with 16 rows and 6/8/6 sts for heel turning (see page 119). Decrease for gusset on every other round until 40 sts rem.

Work sts on ndls 1 and 4 in stockinette for sole and on ndls 2 and 3 in charted pattern for instep. Finish with a band toe (see page 121). Turn sock inside out and join sole and instep sts with three-needle bind-off. Weave in all yarn tails neatly on WS. Make the other sock the same way.

FINISHING
Cut out a paper template the same size as the sole and wrap in plastic wrap. Slip this into the sock foot so that it lies flat. Put the leg into a glass with the sole lying flat on top. This prevents the liquid latex from running. Place the cookie cutter on the sole and fill evenly with ABS-Latex so that no part of the sock inside the cookie cutter can be seen. Allow the sole to set for about 2 hours and then carefully remove the cookie cutter. Make a mirror image for the second sock. Be sure to let both socks dry completely.

Hedgehog Shoes

LEVEL OF DIFFICULTY
Easy

SIZES
18-24 months (approx)
(see page 127 for size measurements)

MATERIALS
Yarn: Schachenmayr Wash+Felt-It! Fine (100% wool, 50 g, 109 yds / 100 m) ruby (106)

Regia Pompon 6-ply (32% polyamide, 43% new wool, 25% polyester, 50 g, 170 yds / 155 m) natural/earth (276)

Needles: circular U.S. size 8 / 5 mm; set of 5 dpn U.S. size 2.5 / 3 mm

Crochet hook: U.S. size C / 2.5 mm

GAUGE
16 sts and 22 rows before felting = 4 x 4 in / 10 x 10 cm.

24 sts and 36 rows after felting = 4 x 4 in / 10 x 10 cm.

Adjust needle size to obtain correct gauge.

STITCH PATTERNS

STOCKINETTE
Worked back and forth: Knit on RS and purl on WS.
In the round: Knit all rounds.

GARTER STITCH
Garter Stitch worked back and forth: Knit all rows.
Garter Stitch in the round: Alternately knit 1 rnd and purl 1 rnd.

INSTRUCTIONS

Begin on sole at toe. With ruby and larger (circular) ndl, CO 6 sts and work back and forth in stockinette. On every other row, at each side, increase 2 sts one time and 1 st 2 times = 14 sts. Work 18 rows in stockinette for the sole. Next, CO 7 sts at each side = 28 sts and work then 22 rows in stockinette. Divide the sts evenly over 2 ndls (= 14 sts per needle) and join with Kitchener st (see page 122). With smaller needles and natural/earth, pick up and knit sts at front of sole: 13 sts on each side and 14 sts on rounded end = 40 sts. Work back and forth in garter sts for 10 rows.
Row 11: Decrease by knitting together sts 11 and 12, 14 and 15, 17 and 18, 20 and 21, 23 and 24, 26 and 27, 29 and 30 = 33 sts rem.
Row 13: Decrease by knitting together sts 12 and 13, 15 and 16, 18 and 19, 21 and 22 = 29 sts rem.
Row 15: Decease by knitting together sts 11 and 12, 13 and 14, 16 and 17, 18 and 19 = 25 sts rem.
Row 17: Decrease by knitting together sts 10 and 11, 12, 13, and 14 (= k3tog), 15 and 16 = 21 sts rem.
Row 18: BO all sts and seam center front of instep.

FELTING
Wash shoes at 104°F / 40°C (see page 125) and pull into shape.

FINISHING
Make 4 cords. With natural/earth, ch 45, turn and work back in sc. Securely stitch cords to top of instep on felted shoe, threading through 12th row.

Prince Charming

LEVEL OF DIFFICULTY
Experienced

SIZES
12-18 months(approx)

(see page 127 for size measurements)

MATERIALS
Yarn: Regia 4-ply, 50 g fern (1092)

Regia Design Line 4-ply (75% wool/25% poly-amide, 50 g, 230 yds/210 m) landscape (4259)

Needles: set of 5 dpn U.S. size 0-2.5 / 2-3 mm; cable needle

GAUGE
28 sts and 36 rows in stockinette = 4 x 4 in / 10 x 10 cm.

Adjust needle size to obtain correct gauge.

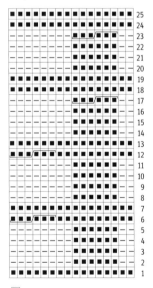

☐ = Knit 1 on RS; purl 1 on WS

■ = Purl 1 on RS; knit 1 on WS

■■■■/■■■ = Place 3 sts on cable ndl behind work, k3 and then k3 from cable ndl

STITCH PATTERNS

RIBBING
K1, p1 around or across.

STOCKINETTE
Worked back and forth: Knit on RS and purl on WS.

In the round: Knit all rounds.

INSTRUCTIONS

With landscape 4, CO 40 sts loosely and divide evenly over dpn; join, being careful not to twist cast-on row. Work 10 rnds in k1/p1 ribbing and then 22 rnds stockinette. Work Dutch heel over 20 sts on ndls 1 and 4 with 16 rows and 6/8/6 sts for heel turning (see page 119). Decrease for gusset on every other round until 40 sts rem. Work

26 rnds in stockinette after completing heel. Finish with band toe (see page 121). Turn sock inside out, divide sts over 2 needles and join with three-needle bind-off.

For the cuff, CO 18 sts and purl 1 row. Work following charted pattern adding an edge st on both sides of the cuff. On WS rows, work sts as they appear (knit the knits and purl the purls). Work Rows 1-25 of chart 3 times but do not bind off. Fold the cuff in half, right sides together. Align the CO edge with the live sts on the ndl and finish with three-needle bind-off. Cut yarn leaving a 1-yd / 1-meter tail.

Sew or knit the cuff onto the sock. Be sure that the seam is hidden under the cuff. Weave in all yarn tails neatly on WS. Make the other sock the same way.

Simply Paradise

STITCH PATTERNS

RIBBING
K1, p1 around or across.

STOCKINETTE
Worked back and forth: Knit on RS and purl on WS.
In the round: Knit all rounds.

INSTRUCTIONS

EDGING OF ROLLED BANDS
Begin the first band by casting on 48 sts with dark brown, join, being careful not to twist cast-on row and divide over 4 dpn. Knit 12 rnds. Cut yarn and set piece aside. With second set of dpn and leaf green, CO 48, join, and knit 8 rnds. Join the two bands by placing the first band inside the second (WS faces WS), with the sets of dpn parallel all around. With leaf green, knit first st of band 1 together with the first st of band 2 and continuing joining the sets of sts all around. Continue with leaf green and work 10 rnds in k1/p1 ribbing.

LEG AND HEEL
Work 26 rounds with leaf green for the leg and then make a short row heel (see page 118). Work the first half of the heel with leaf green, cut yarn, and work the second half with dark brown.

FOOT AND TOE
Knit 35 rounds with brown for the foot and then work the 3-row pattern following the chart. There should be 12 sts on each of the four dpn (pattern repeat = 4 sts); cut leaf green. Knit 2 rnds with dark brown and then work band toe (see page 121).

SNAKE
The snake is made with an I-cord. With Sock Monster, CO 6 sts onto 1 dpn. Knit across but do not turn. Slide sts back to front of left needle, bring yarn behind knitting and knit across; pull yarn a bit at beg of row to tighten braid. Continue until cord is about 14½ in / 37 cm long. Turn and purl back. On next RS row, inc 1 st at each side. Work 5 rows in stockinette, increasing 1 st at each side on every RS row. On the next RS row: ssk after the edge st at beg of row and k2tog before edge st at end of row. Continue in stockinette, decreasing as before on every RS row until 3 sts rem. On next WS row, p3tog, cut yarn and bring tail through last stitch. Make 1 snake for each sock.

3
2
1

■ = k1 dark brown
□ = k1 leaf green

LEVEL OF DIFFICULTY
Experienced

SIZES
2-3 yrs (approx)

(see page 127 for size measurements)

MATERIALS
Yarn: Regia 4-ply (75% wool/25% polyamide, 50 g, 230 yds / 210 m) leaf green(2082) and dark brown (2903)

Regia 4-ply Flusi Color (75% wool/25% poly-amide, 50 g, 229 yds/209 m) Sock Monster (1803)

Needles: 2 sets of 5 dpn U.S. size 0-2.5 / 2-3 mm

Tapestry needle

Sewing thread, green and dark brown

Sewing needle

GAUGE
30 sts and 42 rows in stockinette = 4 x 4 in / 10 x 10 cm.

Adjust needle size to obtain correct gauge.

... Jungle Sock

LEAF

With leaf green, CO 3 sts and work 2 rows in stockinette. Next, work as follows (edge sts are always knitted):

Row 1: Edge st, yo, k1, yo, edge st.

Row 2 and all even-numbered rows: Edge st, purl to last st, edge st.

Row 3: Edge st, k1, yo, k1, yo, k1, edge st.

Row 5: Edge st, k2, yo, k1, yo, k2, edge st.

After completing row 5, work another 7 rows in stockinette. Continue in stockinette shaping leaf by decreasing on every RS row: Edge st, k2tog, knit until 3 sts rem, ssk, edge st. Decrease until 5 sts rem. On the following row knit the 3 center sts tog through back loops. Purl rem 3 sts tog on next row, cut yarn and pull tail through last st. Make 2 leaves for each sock. Lightly steam press leaves so they lie flat.

FINISHING

Weave in all tails neatly on WS. Attach the tail end of the snake under the lower rolled band and then spiral the snake around the leg, sewing it down with green sewing thread. The head of the snake rests on the instep. Sew down the head with brown sewing thread. Attach the leaves as invisibly as possible with green thread arranging them so that the snake peaks out from under each leaf.

Make the second sock to match (mirror imaging spiraling of snake around leg).

If desired, knit the snake for one sock in a different colorway.

Dancing Ducks
Instructions on pages 100-101

Dancing Ducks

LEVEL OF DIFFICULTY
Experienced

SIZES
2-3 yrs (approx)

(see page 127 for size measurements)

Materials

Yarn: Regia 4-ply (75% wool/25% polyamide, 50 g, 230 yds / 210 m) yellow (2041) and Jaffa orange (1259); small amount knitting yarn or wool, black and white

Needles: set of 5 dpn U.S.size 0-2.5 / 2-3 mm

Tapestry needle

GAUGE
30 sts and 42 rows in stockinette = 4 x 4 in / 10 x 10 cm.

Adjust needle size to obtain correct gauge.

STITCH PATTERNS

RIBBING
K1tbl, p1 around or across.

STOCKINETTE
Worked back and forth: Knit on RS and purl on WS.
In the round: Knit all rounds.

INSTRUCTIONS

With yellow, CO 48 sts; divide sts evenly over dpn and join, being careful not to twist cast-on row. Purl 1 rnd. Now work cuff: (with Jaffa orange, knit 1 rnd, purl 1 rnd; with yellow, knit 1 rnd, purl 1 rnd) 4 times. Cut orange and continue with yellow. Purl 2 rnds, so that the cuff will be easier to fold over later. Reverse the cuff so that the inside is now facing out. Continue working on this side so that when you fold the cuff over, the more attractive side will show.
Work 10 rnds in ribbing.

LEG AND HEEL
Knit 38 rnds in stockinette with yellow for the leg and then work Dutch heel (see page 119). Work 24 rows in stockinette for the heel flap alternating 2 rows Jaffa orange and 2 rows yellow. Cut orange and turn heel with yellow.

FOOT AND TOE (BILL)
Continue with yellow. Decrease for gusset on every third rnd until 48 sts rem and then work 23 rnds in stockinette. Work the duck's bill as follows (the round begins at center back). Twist colors around each other on WS every 2 sts to avoid long floats. Make sure that strands do not pull in.
Rnd 1: K4 orange, k16 yellow, k8 orange, k16 yellow, k4 orange.
Rnd 2: K6 orange, k12 yellow, k12 orange, k12 yellow, k6 orange.
Rnd 3: K8 orange, k8 yellow, k16 orange, k8 yellow, k8 orange.
Rnd 4: K10 orange, k4 yellow, k20 orange, k4 yellow, k10 orange.
Cut yellow and then work 2 rnds with orange. Work band toe (see page 121).

DUCK'S FEET

The duck legs are made with I-cords. With orange and dpn, CO 6 sts and knit across; do not turn. Slide sts to front of ndl and knit, pulling yarn when working first st to close gap at back. When I-cord is 1½ in / 3.5 cm long, begin foot. Turn and purl back. On next RS row, M1 after 1st and before last st of row. Continue in stockinette, increasing at each side on every 4th row 3 times. After the final increase, work 3 rows in stockinette and, on next RS row, decrease inside edge sts: ssk at beg of row and k2tog at end. Continue in stockinette, deceasing at each side on every 4th row 3 times. When the last decrease row has been worked, purl 1 row and then BO on next RS row.

With WS facing WS, sew seam foot.

Sew top of I-cord to side of sock just below cuff.

Make two legs for each sock.

TAIL

Make a 1¼ in / 3 cm wide pompon for the tail (see page 127).

FINISHING

Weave in all yarn tails neatly on WS. Fold cuff so that cast-on row meets bottom edge of ribbing. Sew the pompon to back of leg just below the cuff. Embroider the eyes in satin stitch (see page 126) using black yarn and embroider the nostrils in black with straight stitch.

Make the other sock the same way.

High Speed Chase

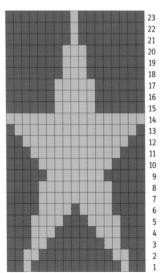

LEVEL OF DIFFICULTY
Easy

SIZES
9-12 months (approx)

(see page 127 for size measurements)

Details for the girls sock are outside the parentheses and those for the boys are within parentheses.

MATERIALS
Yarn: Schachenmayr Universa (55% Merino wool, 45% Acrylic, 50 g, 137 yds / 125 m) pink (36) and cherry (32) for girls sock and lagoon (67) and jade (76) for boys

Needles: set of 5 dpn U.S. size 1.5 / 2.5 mm

Notions: Elastic cord, 31½ in / 80 cm long, bi-color: red/pink for girls and light blue/dark blue for boys

2 cord stoppers, red for girls and green for boys

Liquid latex, ammonia-free: red for girls and white for boys

GAUGE
20 sts and 30 rnds in stockinette = 4 x 4 in / 10 x 10 cm.

Adjust needle size to obtain correct gauge.

STITCH PATTERNS

STOCKINETTE
Worked back and forth: Knit on RS and purl on WS.
In the round: Knit all rounds.

STRIPE SEQUENCE 1
Alternate 1 row pink, 1 row cherry.

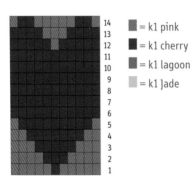

14
13
12
11
10
9
8
7
6
5
4
3
2
1

⬛ = k1 pink
⬛ = k1 cherry
⬛ = k1 lagoon
⬛ = k1 jade

23
22
21
20
19
18
17
16
15
14
13
12
11
10
9
8
7
6
5
4
3
2
1

INSTRUCTIONS

With cherry (lagoon), CO 32 sts. Work 6 rows back and forth in stockinette in stripe sequence 1 (2). Purl 1 row with cherry (lagoon) and then work 5 rows in stockinette and stripe sequence 1 (2).

With another needle, pick up 32 sts from cast-on row. With WS facing WS and needles parallel, join the live and picked-up sts with pink (lagoon): knit together the first st from each needle until all sts have been joined. Now divide sts evenly over dpn and join; work 7 rnds stockinette with pink (lagoon). Make a short row heel with a stitch count of 5/6/5 (see page 118) and then continue in stockinette until foot is 3¾ in / 9.5 cm long. Work band toe (see page 121).

FINISHING
Embroider the heart with cherry (star with jade) in duplicate st, following chart and centering motif on instep (see photos). For each slipper-sock, cut an 11¾-15¾ in / 30-40 cm long piece of elastic cord and thread through casing at top of sock, leaving a 1½ in / 4-cm loop. Use a crochet hook to pull cord through stopper so it is adjustable. To make sure the socks won't slip during wild runs, coat the sole and 1¼ in / 3 cm of toe tip with 5 layers of Latex (see page 126).

Dino Alert

LEVEL OF DIFFICULTY
Intermediate

SIZES
2-3 yrs (approx)

(see page 127 for size measurements)

MATERIALS
Yarn: Regia 4-ply (75% wool/25% polyamide, 50 g, 230 yds / 210 m) Fir (327) and Cherry (2002)

Needles: Set of 5 dpn U.S. size 0-1.5 / 2-2.5 mm

Sewing thread in matching color

Sewing needle

Liquid latex in red

GAUGE
30 sts and 42 rows in stockinette = 4 in x 4 in / 10 x 10 cm.

Adjust needle size to obtain correct gauge.

STITCH PATTERNS

STOCKINETTE
Worked back and forth: Knit on RS and purl on WS.

In the round: Knit all rounds.

INSTRUCTIONS

With fir, CO 48 sts; divide sts over 4 dpn and join, being careful not to twist cast-on row. For the rolled edge, work 10 rnds in st st. Then work 10 rnds in k1/p1 ribbing. Follow basic instructions for the rest of the sock, including short-row heel and band toe (see pages 118, p 121 and the table on page 127).

BACK RIDGE (MAKE 2)
With one needle and cherry, CO 48 sts.

Purl 1 row, knit 1 row; turn.

WS: Work the first st as a slipped yarnover (slyo, see short row heel, page 118), p13, turn.

RS: Work the first st as slyo, k12, turn.

Continue working short rows until, with RS facing, all 14 sts on the ndls are slyo sts (7 on the right hand ndl and 7 on the left hand ndl). You

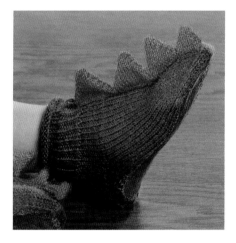

have just completed one side of the first triangle on the ridge. You now have to work back down the other side, from the tip to the base.

RS: K slyo (work slyo as a single knit st), turn.

WS: Sl 1, p slyo (work slyo as a single p st), turn.

RS: Sl 1, k1, k slyo, turn.

WS: Sl 1, p2, p slyo, turn.

Continue in this way to the last row:

WS: Sl 1, p 12, p slyo.

All 14 sts on the right hand ndl are now regular sts. Repeat with the next 14, 12 and 8 sts respectively to complete the ridge. You will need to purl the first st of the first row of each triangle before you can make the slyo. When all 4 triangles are complete, knit 1 row (48 sts) and bind off purlwise.

FINISHING
With matching yarn, sew the straight edges of each ridge to the center of each sock. Finally, apply 5 layers of latex to the sole (see p 126).

Fresh Colors

LEVEL OF DIFFICULTY
Intermediate

SIZE
18-24 months (approx)

(see page 127 for size measurements)

MATERIALS
Yarn: Schachenmayr Baby Soft (60% Acrylic/40% nylon, 25 g, 77 yds / 70 m) confetti spot (1081) and 25 g pink (136)

Needles: set of 5 dpn U.S. size 2.5 / 3 mm

Crochet hook: U.S. size D-3 / 3 mm

GAUGE
22 sts and 30 rows in stockinette = 4 x 4 in / 10 x 10 cm.

Adjust needle size to obtain correct gauge.

STITCH PATTERNS

STOCKINETTE
Worked back and forth: Knit on RS and purl on WS.
In the round: Knit all rounds.

REVERSE STOCKINETTE
Worked back and forth: Purl on RS and knit on WS.
In the round: Purl all rounds.

RIBBING
(P4, k4) across or around.

STRIPE SEQUENCE
1 rnd confetti spot, 4 rnds pink.

INSTRUCTIONS

LEFT SOCK
The leg is worked from side to side. With confetti spot, CO 41 sts and knit 6 rows. On Row 3, work:

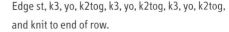

Edge st, k3, yo, k2tog, k3, yo, k2tog, k3, yo, k2tog, and knit to end of row.

Row 7: Edge st, 17 sts in p4, k4 ribbing, 5 sts stockinette, 17 sts ribbing, edge st.

Continue as for Row 7 for 26 rows — center of leg. Work other half of leg to match and then BO all sts. With pink, pick up and knit 40 sts along purl ridge of leg. Divide sts evenly on dpn and join. Knit 6 rnds and then work short row heel over sts on ndls 1 and 2 (see page 118). After completing heel, work 7 rnds with pink and then work in stripe sequence. When foot is 4¼ in / 11 cm long, cut confetti and continue with pink only. Knit 1 rnd and then work star toe (see page 121).

Make the right sock to match, reversing patterning on leg.

FINISHING
Seam the center back of leg and weave in all yarn tails neatly on WS. Crochet a short chain st cord (chain to desired length and then sc back across chain) for each sock and thread through side of leg (see photo for placement). Make 4 small pompons (diameter ¾ in / 2 cm) (see page 127) and securely sew one pompon to each cord end.

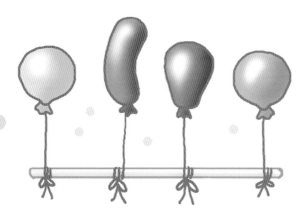

Mini-Harlequin

LEVEL OF DIFFICULTY
Intermediate

SIZE
2-3 yrs (approx)
(see page 127 for size measurements)

MATERIALS
Yarn: Schachenmayr Wash+Felt It! Fine
(100% wool, 50 g, 109 yds / 100 m) olive
(117) and petroleum (107)

Needles: circular U.S. size 8 / 5 mm

Notions: 2 bells, about ³/₈-³/₄ in / 1-2 cm
diameter; sewing thread and needle

GAUGE
16 sts and 22 rows in stockinette = 4 x 4 in /
10 x 10 cm.

24 sts and 36 rows after felting = 4 x 4 in /
10 x 10 cm.

Adjust needle size to obtain correct gauge.

STITCH PATTERN

STOCKINETTE
Worked back and forth: Knit on RS and purl
on WS.
In the round: Knit all rounds.

INSTRUCTIONS

The shoe is made in two sections in stockinette.
With olive, CO 27 sts and work 2 rows in stocki-
nette. To shape the sawtooth edges, at right side
of piece, on every other row, BO 2 sts 3 times.
Next, CO 2 sts at the same edge 3 times. Repeat
the decrease/increase sequence again. After the
last increase row, work 2 rows over all sts.
On right side of piece, BO 11 sts = 16 sts rem.
Work 20 rows and then, the on the right side,
CO 6 sts for the toe tips.
Begin decreasing on Row 23. On every other
row at both sides, BO 1 st 2 times, 2 sts 2 times,
and 3 sts 1 time. BO rem 4 sts.
Work the other side of the shoe to match with
petroleum, increasing and decreasing on left
side of piece. Seam two pieces together, one of
each color, along back, under sole, and around
tip of instep.
Make the other shoe to match, reversing color
arrangement.

FELTING
Wash shoes at 104°F / 40°C (see page 125) and
pull into shape.

FINISHING
Sew on bells securely.

A Cossack on Tour

LEVEL OF DIFFICULTY
Intermediate

SIZE
2-3 yrs (approx)
(see page 127 for size measurements)

MATERIALS
Yarn: Schachenmayr Wash+Felt It! Fine
(100% wool, 50 g, 109 yds / 100 m)
2-pink (111)

Regia 4-ply Color (75% wool, 25% polyamide, 50 g, 230 yds / 210 m) Sock Monster
(1803)

Needles: circular and set of 5 dpn U.S. size
8 / 5 mm

Straight ndls U.S. size 1.5 / 2.5 mm

Crochet hook: U.S. size B or C / 2.5 mm

Notions: 4 large-hole beads, about ¾ in /
2 cm diameter

GAUGE
16 sts and 22 rows in stockinette = 4 x 4 in /
10 x 10 cm.

24 sts and 36 rows after felting = 4 x 4 in /
10 x 10 cm.

Adjust needle size to obtain correct gauge.

STITCH PATTERNS

STOCKINETTE
Worked back and forth: Knit on RS and purl
on WS.
In the round: Knit all rounds.

GARTER STITCH
Garter Stitch worked back and forth: Knit all sts.
Garter Stitch in the round: Alternately knit 1 rnd
and purl 1 rnd.

INSTRUCTIONS

With pink and U.S. 8 / 5 mm ndls, CO 70 sts and
work 8 rows in stockinette. To make the slit at
each side, BO 7 sts at each side 6 times and then
CO 7 sts at each side 6 times. Work 10 rows in
stockinette stitch and then place the first 17 sts
and the last 17 sts on a holder.
Divide the rem 36 sts evenly onto U.S. 8 / 5 mm
dpn (9 sts on each of 4 dpn) and join. Work 28
rnds in stockinette and then begin toe. On every
rnd, k2tog at beg of each dpn until 2 sts rem per
dpn. Cut yarn and thread tail through rem 8 sts;
pull tight and weave in tail neatly on WS. Join the
2 sets of 17 sts with Kitchener st. Seam back.
With Sock Monster, work 2 rows in single crochet
(42 sc around slit). Make the other shoe the
same way.

FELTING
Wash shoes at 104°F / 40°C (see page 125) and
pull into shape.

FINISHING
Work the inset with Sock Monster in garter st.
With smaller ndls, CO 3 sts and work 3 rows in
garter st. On the 4th row, work up to the center
stitch. From the center stitch, increase as follows:
k1 (leaving st on the ndl), yo, k1, continue to end.
Work this increase every 4th row until there are
19 stitches on the needle. Work 6 more rows and
bind off. Attach the edges of inset to the slit with
crochet. Make 4 tassels and thread a bead over
each (see photo). Securely sew each tassel to slit.

Off to the Playing Field!

LEVEL OF DIFFICULTY
Intermediate

SIZE
2-3 yrs (approx)

(see page 127 for size measurements)

MATERIALS
Yarn: Schachenmayr Wash+Felt It! Fine (100% wool, 50 g, 109 yds / 100 m) 2-white (102) and 2-azure (113)

Needles: Circular and set of 5 dpn U.S. size 8 / 5 mm

Crochet Hook: U.S. size H-8 / 5 mm

Liquid Latex, white

GAUGE
16 sts and 22 rows in stockinette = 4 x 4 in / 10 x 10 cm.

24 sts and 36 rows after felting = 4 x 4 in / 10 x 10 cm.

Adjust needle size to obtain correct gauge.

STITCH PATTERNS

STOCKINETTE
Worked back and forth: Knit on RS and purl on WS.
In the round: Knit all rounds.

GARTER STITCH
Garter Stitch worked back and forth: Knit all sts.

INSTRUCTIONS

Holding 2 strands of white together and with circular ndl, begin at the sole by casting on 6 sts. Work back and forth in stockinette. On row 3, increase 1 st with M1 inside edge st at each side. Continue in stockinette over these 8 sts until there are 30 rows total. To round front, on every other row decrease 1 st at each side 2 times and then BO rem 4 sts. Now use a single strand of white to pick up and knit sts, beginning at center back: 5 sts over heel, 26 sts on each side and 14 sts at front tip and another 5 sts on other side of heel = total of 76 sts. Join and purl 1 rnd and then knit 7 rnds. Cut yarn. Now work back and forth in garter st over the center 20 sts for instep.
Row 3: Dec with k2tog on sts 2 and 3, 5 and 6, 8 and 9, 12 and 13, 15 and 16, 18 and 19 = 14 sts rem.
Row 5: Edge st, (k2tog) 6 times, edge st = 8 sts rem.
Row 7: Edge st, (k2tog) 3 times, edge st = 5 sts rem.
Row 9: Edge st, k3tog tbl, edge st = 3 sts rem.
Row 10: K3tog tbl; cut yarn.
Divide the rem 56 sts over 4 dpn. Begin at center back; attach azure. Work around in stockinette and short rows. At each side, work 1 x 4 sts, 1x 2 sts, and leave 8 x 1 st unworked. Work the short row heel with slyo sts (see short row heel page 118) turn = 28 sts. Do not cut yarn.
With azure, pick up and knit 10 sts at the edge of the white toe cap. Work back and forth in rows, joining the sections as you work: on RS ssk and on WS purl the first or last sts together with 1 st from side respectively, until there are 28 + 10 sts remaining. Cut yarn.
Now continue working in the round, beg at center back, with the strand on hold. Knit 1 rnd, then purl 1 rnd and at the same time, BO. For the shoe strings, with white and crochet hook, ch 100; cut yarn and pull tail through last chain st. Thread chain through instep (see photo).

Make other shoe the same way.

FELTING
Wash shoes at 104°F / 40°C (see page 125) and pull into shape.

FINISHING
When shoes are completely dry, paint on a star at outside of each shoe with liquid latex (see photo for placement of stars).

Basic Instructions

This might be your first pair of socks, no problem! Here is where you'll find the illustrated descriptions of all the basic techniques you'll need to knit socks. With the help of the photos and detailed explanations, even beginners can get started with no problem. You'll learn how to knit heels and toes, work Kitchener stitch, and embellish with crochet and embroidery. You'll also find explanations for felting and applying latex soles. A large table of sizes for baby shoes up to size 25 makes it easy to find the right size for every child. This book is also a good reference for the experienced knitter.

KNITTING

ABBREVIATIONS

beg	begin, beginning
BO	bind off
CC	contrast color
Cm	centimeter(s)
CO	cast on
dpn	double-pointed needle(s)
g	gram(s)
in	inch(es)
k	knit
k1f&b	knit into front and then back of same stitch
k2tog	knit two stitches together
m	meter(s)
M1	make 1 = lift strand between 2 sts and knit into back loop
MC	main color
mm	millimeter(s)
ndl(s)	needle(s)
p	purl
psso	pass slipped stitch over
rem	remain, remaining
rep	repeat
rnd(s)	round(s)
RS	right side
sc	single crochet
sl	slip
ssk	slip, slip, knit = (slip 1 knitwise) 2 times and knit together through back loops
st(s)	stitch(es)
tbl	through back loop
WS	wrong side
wyb	with yarn held in back

LONG-TAIL CAST ON

The long-tail cast on is one of the most widely used for many reasons. It is quick and easy to learn, it produces a firm, yet stretchy edge, and it is as attractive on the right side as it is on the wrong side. The tail should be at least three times as long as the circumference of the sock. Make a slip knot on your needle and hold it in your right hand. This will count as your first stitch. In your left hand, wrap the ball yarn (the yarn which is attached to the skein) around your index finger and the tail end of your yarn around your thumb. Secure both strands in your palm with your other fingers controlling the tension. The needle and the slip knot should be held between the outstretched strands between the thumb and forefinger, as shown.

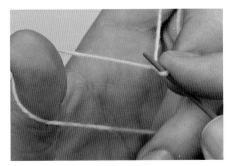

Insert the needle from below and pick up the front (or foremost) thumb strand.

Pull the strand through the thumb loop.

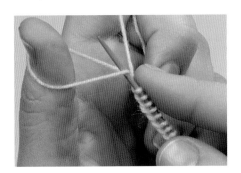

Continue upward and guide the needle over the top of the strand held on the index finger.

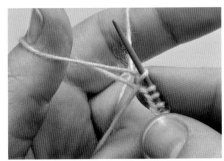

Finally, remove your thumb from the loop and let it drop. Place your thumb back under the tail and gently tighten up the stitch on the needle. Avoid pulling too tight! Continue in this way until the desired number of stitches has been cast on.

PROVISIONAL/TUBULAR CAST ON

This provisional/tubular cast on with waste yarn results in an extra stitch which is decreased/eliminated in the transition round. With this variation, the stitches are built around a 24 in / 60 cm length of waste yarn. Make a slip knot with the ball yarn a few inches from the end and place it on the needle. Leave the tail long enough so that it will be easy to weave in later when finishing. Hold one end of the waste yarn next to the slip knot in your right hand. The ball yarn is held over the index finger of your left hand and the waste yarn is held over the thumb.

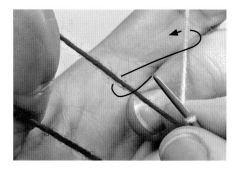

First, bring the needle forward and under the waste yarn, then over the top of the ball yarn in a "figure eight" motion, grab a loop and bring it down, under the waste yarn.

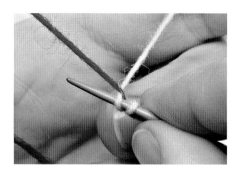

Second, make a yarnover by guiding the needle under the ball yarn and up and over the top. Repeat these two steps until you have the desired number of stitches.

To stabilize the last loop, bring one more stitch under the waste yarn. This stitch will be decreased in the third round as you transition to the cuff. Afterwards, work 6 transition rounds and attach to it a cuff of either 1x1 or 2x2 ribbing. Once the cuff is complete, you can pull out the waste yarn.

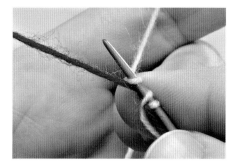

TRANSITION TO THE CUFF FOR BOTH CAST ON VARIATIONS WITH AN EXTRA STITCH

Turn your work and continue working back and forth in rows.

Row 1: Knit the knit stitches, slip purl stitch with yarn in front, turn.

Row 2: Knit the knits, slip purl stitch with yarn in front. Now divide the stitches evenly between the four needles and connect the round.

Round 3: Purl the purl stitches, slip the knit stitches with the yarn in back. Knit the extra stitch on the fourth needle together with the 1st stitch on the first needle.

Round 4: Knit the knit stitches, slip the purl stitches with yarn in front.

Rounds 5 and 6: Repeat rounds 3 and 4.

SHORT ROW HEEL

The short row heel is worked in two stages, in rows back and forth on the stitches of needles 1 and 4. The short row heel is shorter than the dutch heel. When you get 1-2 cm before the end of the leg, work the stitches on needles 1 and 4 in stockinette stitch and the stitches on needles 2 and 3 in the texture pattern. This way you can easily decrease any extra stitches on needles 1 and 4. In the first stage, divide the heel stitches in to 3 sections. Then work short rows with so called "slipped yarnovers" (slyo) over the outer two thirds of stitches beginning with the outer-most stitches of the first or fourth needles. (Slipped yarn overs make it possible to knit a short row heel with no holes.):

Row 1 (right side): Work all stitches including the last stitch of the first needle in stockinette stitch, turn.

Row 2 (wrong side): Work a slipped yarnover (slyo). With yarn in front as if to purl, slip the next stitch as if to purl. Wrap the yarn over the top of the right-hand needle and pull tightly so that the two legs of the stitch from the row below are stretched over the needle. If the yarn is not pulled tightly enough, you will eventually see a hole in your work. Purl all remaining stitches including the last stitch on needle four.

Row 3 (right side): Work a slyo, then knit all stitches up to the slyo at the end of the row (the slyo remains unworked), turn.

Row 4 (wrong side): Work a slyo, then purl all stitches up to the slyo at the end of the row, turn.

Repeat rows 3 and 4 until all the stitches in the outer thirds have been worked as slyo stitches. The remaining slyo stitch will be worked in a right side row.

Work two rounds, knitting the heel stitches and working the stitches on needles 3 and 4 in the leg pattern. In the first round, work the slipped yarnovers by carefully inserting your needle under both legs of the stitch. Don't mistake each leg of the stitch for two separate stitches. The second round ends at the beginning of the middle third of stitches.

In the second stage, continue working short rows with slyo stitches, but in the opposite direction, from inner to the outside.

Row 1 (right side): Knit all stitches, including the last stitch of the center third, turn.
Row 2 (wrong side): Work a slyo stitch, purl up to and including the last stitch of the center third, turn.
Row 3: Work a slyo stitch, knit up to the slyo stitch, turn.
Row 4: Work a slyo stitch, purl up to the slyo stitch, turn.

Repeat rows 3 and 4 until all the slyo stitches from the 1st and 3rd thirds have been worked. Resume knitting in the round and follow instructions, as given for pattern. At the beginning of the first round, you'll be working a slyo st.
To work a slipped yarn over, carefully insert your needle under both legs of the stitch. You don't want to mistake each leg of the stitch for two separate stitches.

There is no gusset worked for this type of heel.

DUTCH HEEL

This three-part heel is a classic and the most often used. Advantages of this heel are its simplicity and the ease with which it can be strengthened.

HEEL FLAP
The stitches on needles 2 and 3 are on hold. Place the stitches on needles 1 and 4 together on one needle. They will be worked back and forth to form the heel flap. The edge stitches are worked in garter stitch (knit the first and last stitch of each row). The heel flap is the correct height when you have half as many garter stitch "knots" on both edges as heel stitches, or-and this is the same-as many "knots" as heel stitches on one dpn. Finish halfway through a RS row, at the center of the heel.

TURNING THE HEEL
Now you'll work back and forth on the center third of the heel stitches. Re-arrange your stitches so that the stitches from needles 2 and 3 are on one needle. This is possible here because the heel flap is now longer and won't pull against the stitches on hold as you knit.
Carefully divide the heel stitches into three sections, two outer sections which must be equal the middle section. If the stitch count is not evenly divisible by three, just add the extras to the center section.

Place each set of side stitches on a dpn. The starting point is the center of the heel on a RS row.

The side stitches are on hold. Knit to the center of the heel. The little heel cap is worked on the stitches in the middle section.
Row 1 (half row RS): K up to the last stitch of the middle section, and then, with the last stitch of the middle section and the first stitch of the side section, ssk (left leaning dec), turn.
Row 2 (WS): Sl 1, p up to the last st of the middle section, sl 1, place sl st on left hand needle, p2tog, turn.

Row 3 (RS): Sl 1, k up to last st, ssk, turn.

Repeat rows 2 and 3, continuing to slip the first st of each row and working a decrease with the last stitch of the middle section and the first stitch of the side section, until there are no more sts on the sides and only the middle section is left. Finish with a half RS row to end in the center of the heel.

DECREASING AND GUSSET

After turning the heel, it's time to continue knitting in the round. In the first round, pick up each stitch along the garter stitch borders of the heel flap.

Work an additional round on all needles as follows: work in pattern stitch on needles 2 and 3, work the sole in stockinette stitch on needles 1 and 4 and redistribute the stitches so that the same number are on each one. Place a marker between needles 4 and 1 so that you can tell when a new round starts.

In order to avoid holes on the sides, knit together tbl, the last stitch on ndl 1 and the first stitch on ndl 2 and again the last stitch of needle 3 together with the first needle on needle 4.

Now that the heel has been turned, you must return to the original stitch count by knitting the gusset. This creates some extra room in the instep. When the gusset is complete, you will have returned to the original stitch count.

The starting point of the round is at the beginning of needle 1. When all of the stitches from the heel flap have been decreased, work one more round.

DECREASE ROUND

Needle 1: Knit up to last 3 sts, k2tog (right leaning), k1.

Needles 2 and 3: Knit in pattern.

Needle 4: Knit up to last 3 sts, ssk (left leaning), k1.

Repeat this decrease round every second or third round as necessary until the original stitch count has been reached.

Complete the foot as desired.

BAND TOE

For the band toe, decrease as follows:
Needles 1 and 3: Knit up to the last 3 sts, k2tog, k1
Needles 2 and 4: K1, ssk, knit to end.
Follow directions and continue decreasing until 8 sts rem. Cut strand, draw yarn through last 8 sts twice, secure end.

STAR TOE

The star toe, along with the band toe, are the most used methods for knitting toes. Because the decreases are distributed evenly around the toe, it is a bit more durable and softer than the band toe. If you use a left-leaning decrease, a nice pattern will form. A right-leaning decrease will hardly be visible. For the star toe, you'll need an even stitch count per needle. Extra stitches can be decreased a few rows before the beginning of the toe decrease. Two stitches are decreased per needle on every decrease round. Separate the stitches on each needle into two equal parts (even stitch count).

DECREASE ROUNDS

Knit together the first two stitches of the first half and the first two stitches of the second half of stitches on each needle. The number of straight rounds worked between decrease rounds should be the same as the number of stitches worked between decreases on the following decrease round.
Rule of thumb: Work as many rounds between decreases as stitches between decreases. Continue in this way until 8 stitches remain and cut yarn, pull through rem stitches and secure on the inside with a yarn needle.

KITCHENER STITCH

The Kitchener stitch is used to join two pieces of knitted fabric with a seam that mimics a row of stitches in a matching gauge. With a blunt yarn needle and a length of matching yarn, a seam is created between two parallel rows of live stitches.

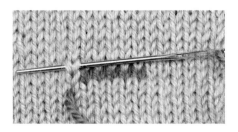

The Kitchener stitch is also used over the top of a piece of knitted fabric when a duplicate stitch is desired.

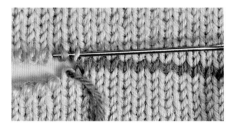

Working the curves of the heel and toe stitches which have yet to be knit is quite tricky. The stitches of the fabric are under greater tension and are quicker to unravel when stretched. If stitches are dropped, return to the last decrease round. If necessary , the dropped stitches may need to be knit up from several rounds down. It is much safer to put the last of the heel and toe stitches onto two parallel dpn with the same number of stitches on each needle. Kitchener stitch is a sort of hybrid of knitting and sewing.

Thread a blunt-tipped yarn needle with a length of matching yarn approximately 20 in long.

Prepare the first stitch:

Insert the yarn needle purlwise into the first stitch on the front needle and pull the yarn through, leaving the stitch on the needle.

Insert the yarn needle knitwise into the first stitch on the back needle and pull the yarn through, leaving the stitch on the needle. Now the stitches can come off the needle:

Step 1: Insert the tapestry needle knitwise into the stitch on the front needle and pull the yarn through, removing the stitch from the needle (= knit off).

Step 2: Insert the tapestry needle purlwise into the next stitch on the front needle and pull the yarn through, leaving the stitch on the needle (= purl).

Step 3: Insert the tapestry needle purlwise into the stitch on the back needle and pull the yarn through, removing the stitch from the needle (= purl off).

Step 4: Insert the tapestry needle knitwise into the next stitch on the back needle and pull the yarn through, leaving the stitch on the needle (= knit).

Give the yarn a little tug after each stitch. Hold the working yarn to the right under the knitting needles. Repeat steps 1-4 until all stitches have been worked. Work steps 1 and 3 for the rem two stitches.

CROCHET

CHAIN STITCH (CH)

Crocheted pieces usually begin with a chain of chain stitch loops and this starting chain provides the base upon which other stitches are formed. For every single crochet stitch that will be worked, you need to make one chain stitch. The lower photo at the center of the page shows the front of the chain. On the back of the chain are little "purl bumps" between each stitch.

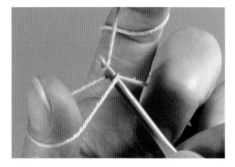

To begin the chain, arrange the yarn around your thumb and forefinger as shown in the top left photo. Insert the hook under the front strand on the thumb and then catch the index finger strand as shown.

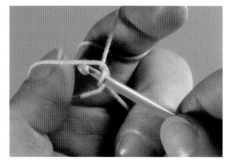

Bring the caught strand forward through the thumb loop, and, at the same time, release the

loop from the thumb and tighten it. Be careful that the strand on the hook doesn't fall off.

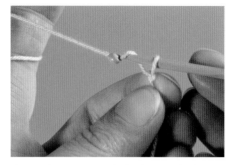

The new loop stays on the hook as you begin the next stitch which will be the first "chain stitch." The hook goes under the strand from the forefinger and then the hook catches the yarn from above and pulls that strand through the loop on the hook.

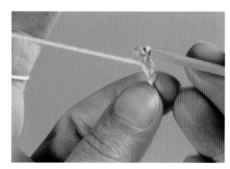

Now you have the first V-shaped "chain stitch" on the hook. Continue making chain stitches by pulling the forefinger strand through the loop on the hook until you have the number needed for your piece. After you have made the necessary number of chain stitches, you can turn and work back across by crocheting into the chain stitches.

SINGLE CROCHET (SC)

Single crochet is a little stitch. You can see in the photo below how compact a single crochet stitch is. The photo with a row of single crochet shows how stitches are typically formed. If you work a second row of single crochet above the first, the stitches will look like little stars or flowers.

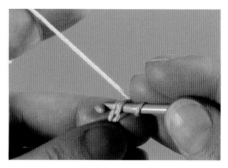

Begin by making a starting chain of chain stitches with the same number as single crochet stitches you will make on the next row + 1. The extra chain stitch is the "turning chain." The first single crochet is worked into the second chain from the hook.

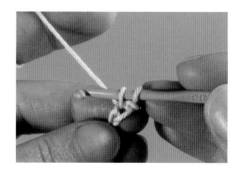

Insert the hook through the chain st from front to back, catch the working strand with the hook and bring the strand through the chain st. Now there are 2 loops on the hook.

CRAB STITCH

Crab stitch is a single crochet stitch worked in the opposite direction, that is, from left to right. Begin by inserting hook from front to back through both loops at top of sc in previous row.

PICOT

A picot is a small, ingenious and decorative stitch made with chain loops along an edge. Usually picot stitches are made between single crochet stitches. Begin with *1 sc into a single crochet stitch of row below and then chain 4.

Bring the yarn around the hook and through both loops = 1 single crochet stitch completed. Work one single crochet in each chain stitch across, working from right to left across chain.

Catch the working yarn and bring through the stitch loops. Notice that the loops on the hook are twisted. Now catch the yarn around the hook and pull it through both loops on the hook. Crab stitch makes a corded edging.

Now make 1 single crochet stitch into the 4th chain from hook. Skip one sc and repeat from * to make a picot in the next sc.

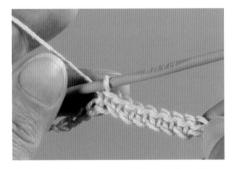

At the end of the row, turn with chain 1 and then work another row of single crochet, beginning in the 2nd sc from the hook.

FELTING

GAUGE SWATCH

Before beginning any knitting project, you should knit a gauge swatch. Always use the same needle size as that given for the largest part of the garment.

Schachenmayr Wash and Felt-It!:
Work a gauge swatch with size US 11 / 8 mm needles in stockinette stitch, unfelted: 11.5 stitches and 17 rows = 4 x 4 in / 10 x 10 cm felted: 24 sts and 36 rows = 4 x 4 in / 10 x 10 cm

KNITTING

Begin knitting shoes at the heel. Cast on according to the size chart, and knit back and forth in rows. Then arrange stitches on dpn as directed and in the first round, before connecting the round, make 2 stitches. The first of the two new stitches goes on the needle before and the second stitch on the next needle. Work in the round on the number of stitches as indicated in the chart. For the toe, knit together the first 2 stitches of each needle until only 2 stitches rem on each needle. Cut strand, pull end through rem 8 sts and secure on the inside of the work. Sew the heel seam as smoothly as possible.

WASHING AND FELTING

The shoes should be washed in the machine on "hot". Do not use any water-saving or delicate wash features. Place one pair of shoes per load with half the usual amount of soap. The shoes need to be fully submerged in water or they will not felt properly. Add three tennis balls to the load to add friction. As soon as the washing is complete, place the heel of the shoe over your fist to make it nice and round! If, by chance, the shoe is still too large, try washing it once more on "warm".

TIPS AND TRICKS

- This style of shoe is very comfortable. For smaller feet, you can leave out the addition of the two extra stitches in front.
- If knitting stripes, always change color at the center of the sole so the color change is not noticeable.
- For a perfect heel seam, cast on with a waste yarn in a contrasting color. Remove this strand at the end, divide the stitches in half and place each half on a dpn. Finish the seam in Kitchener stitch.
- The shoes can be made non-slip by applying iron-on "ABS-Stopper". You can also apply latex to the sole once the shoe is dry, for the same effect (see p 126).

APPLYING THE LATEX SOLE

Cut out 2 copies of a thick paper template the same size as the sole and wrap in plastic wrap. Slip this into the sock foot so that it lies flat. Stir the latex thoroughly with a spoon, but be careful not to let it get foamy. Paint the sole of the sock evenly with a brush. For an active child and the greatest amount of traction, be sure to cover the entire sole completely. If the shoes will only be worn a few hours a day, it is nicer if the latex is applied in stripes, spots, or some other pattern. This allows the feet to breathe better! Allow the first layer of latex to dry thoroughly. If possible, use a blow dryer for a few minutes until the latex is clear. An oven at 167 deg F / 75 deg C is also a possibility. The next layer is easier to apply if you paint it on with 1 in strips of sponge.

Apply a minimum of 5 layers, always allowing the top layer to dry completely before applying the next one. Allow the finished sole to dry overnight.

Latex makes the bristles of the brush adhere to one another so it cannot be used again.

EMBROIDERY STITCHES

"STRAIGHT STITCH"

STEM STITCH

SATIN STITCH

CHAIN KNOT

FRENCH KNIT STITCH

DAISY STITCH

THIS IS ONLY A GENERAL GUIDELINE AS BABIES COME IN ALL SIZES

INFANT AND TODDLER SOCK SIZES FOR REGIA 4-PLY

Sizes by age (approx)	0-3 months			3-6 months	6-9 months	9-12 months	3-6 months	12-18 months	2-3 years
Number of sts to CO/sts per ndl	28/7	32/8	36/9	36/9	40/10	40/10	44/11	44/11	48/12
Heel band stitch count	14	16	18	18	20	20	22	22	24
Stitch count for short row heel	4/6/4	5/6/5	6/6/6	6/6/6	6/8/6	6/8/6	7/8/7	7/8/7	8/8/8
Length of foot from mid-heel to tip of toe	2.25"	2.5"	2.75"	3"	3.25"	3.75"	4.25"	4.5"	5"
Number of additional decreases for the band toe after the first decrease (no #s in this row)									
In the 3rd round	1x	1x	1x	1x	1x	1x	1x	1x	1x
In the 2nd round	2x	2x	2x	3x	3x	3x	3x	3x	3x
In every round	1x	2x	3x	2x	3x	3x	4x	4x	5x
Total length in inches	3"	3.25"	3.75"	4"	4.25"	5"	5.25"	5.75"	6.25"

POM POMS

1. Using a compass, draw a circle of the desired circumference on a piece of cardboard. Draw a smaller circle in the center and cut it out. Make another so that you have two identical cardboard "donuts".

2. Place the cardboard pieces together and wrap—always from inside to outside—with yarn until the pieces are completely covered.

3. With a scissors, cut around the outside of the circle.

4. Slide a length of yarn between the circles, pull tight and tie a knot.

5. Pull the circles off and trim the pompom so that it is even on all sides.

YARN SUPPLIERS

Westminster Fibers
165 Ledge Street
Nashua, NH 03060
800-445-9276
www.westminsterfibers.com

Webs – America's Yarn Store
75 Service Center Road
Northampton, MA 01060
800-367-9327
www.yarn.com
customerservice@yarn.com

The Yarn Barn (Kirtland's)
5077 Andersonville Road
Dillwyn, VA 23936
800-850-6008
www.yarnbarn.com
info@yarnbarn.com

For more information on selecting or substitut-
ing yarn contact your local yarn shop or an online
store, they are familiar with all types of yarns
and would be happy to help you. Additionally,
the online knitting community at Ravelry.com
has forums where you can post questions about
specific yarns. Yarns come and go so quickly
these days and there are so many beautiful
yarns available.